Advance Praise for
I Am Enough

"Donna lays bare her soul in this stirring and thoroughly engrossing read. She takes us along on her journey from small town girl to pioneering female minister, giving us access along the way to the deepest wells of personal struggle and self-doubt that most of us would sooner run and hide from, much less publish for the world to see, as Donna has so bravely and graciously done for us in *I Am Enough*. And we are the better for it. Donna's inspiring story is a gift that will touch readers of any age and give a richly informed perspective on the human spirit in its search of ultimate meaning, truth, and joy."
—*Dustin Lance Black, Academy Award-Winning Screenwriter*

"Whitehead has written a thoughtful spiritual autobiography that is honest and inspiring. With transparency and vulnerability, she weaves together her own spiritual journey, the stories of two leading churches in America, and the work of the Holy Spirit in such a compelling way that I could not put it down."
—*Adam Hamilton, Pastor and Author of*
Wrestling with Doubt, Finding Faith

"Rev. Donna Whitehead's *I Am Enough* offers a powerful and timely message of hope, purpose, and the enduring love of God, particularly relevant for young clergywomen of color who often navigate spaces that challenge their worth and sense of belonging. Rooted in both scriptural truth and contemporary analysis, Donna encourages churches and individuals to reclaim their God-given missions, moving beyond fear, division, and scarcity. In a world that often marginalizes and divides, the affirmation that "we are enough" is transformative. This book is a must-read for any

clergywoman, particularly those who feel overwhelmed by the demands of ministry or the weight of societal pressures. It is a bold declaration that in God's eyes, we are enough, and through His love, we are empowered to make an extraordinary impact on the world around us."
—*Christina Winbush Hardy, Campus Minister, Texas A&M University at Commerce Wesley Foundation*

"Donna Whitehead is a colleague whom I've served beside for a quarter of a century. I am but one who could say I have never witnessed anyone who joyfully experiences ministry more than Donna Whitehead. For those who know Donna, they smile at her positive approach to life and her love for learning. *I Am Enough* is a story that had to be told from a lifelong learner who could definitely be a teacher, expert, or authority on the subject of women in ordained ministry. The tenor of *I Am Enough* at times reads like an appealing memoir; the overall impression of the book, however, is one of a humbly presented testimony to learning and growing in God's grace and through life-changing revelation."
—*Stan Copeland, Senior Pastor Lovers Lane UMC, Dallas*

"This is one of the best spiritual autobiographies I have ever read! Donna is a storyteller and accomplished writer; both make for a good read. However, what really makes this book stand out is not just its down-home style, but the journey of calling and career that are marked by personal growth, insight, and committed transparency and vulnerability. My late wife Ursula and I first met Donna in the summer of 2015. We had requested a meeting to see if a professor from the other seminary in Dallas would fit in at Lovers Lane UMC. Not only were we welcomed, but Donna encouraged us both to use our teaching gifts to strengthen the church. We never looked back."
—*W. Hall Harris III, ThM, PhD, Senior Professor of NT Studies (ret.), Dallas Theological Seminary*

"Donna's new memoir shares the wisdom that has guided her through a remarkable life: 'There is always something to learn.' I have known Donna as a mentor and colleague for over nine years, and I've seen first-hand how her life has been a testament to the power of continual growth and resilience. This book goes beyond mere words, as she shares her journey of a life well-lived, where every challenge is met with the opportunity to learn and thrive. I know you will enjoy Donna's story as she reveals the lessons learned from a life of rich experiences and unending curiosity."
—*DeDe Jones, Associate Pastor of Modern Worship and Evangelism, Lovers Lane UMC*

"Donna is a spiritual seeker who, in her study of adult development, Jungian psychology, and insights into self-development through the Enneagram, along with her continuing study of Scripture and pastoral work, realized that her true Self could only be realized by letting go of ego-driven goals. She shares openly the ongoing necessity of personal willingness to go deeper within, as well as expanding her love and ministry in more inclusive dimensions than numbers and accomplishments. Her tone even becomes confessional in the service of being clear about the challenges we (and the church) have to face to move forward in becoming truly Christian community. She has discovered and here proclaims the wisdom of Irenaeus: 'The Glory of God is Humanity Fully Alive.'"
—*Betsy Alden, Visiting Professor, Founding Director of Service-Learning, Program in Education, Duke University*

"I hope that both women and men—clergy and laypersons of all denominations—will read, enjoy, and learn from Donna's story of what it has been like to be a woman in ministry through decades of challenges and changes. Her memoir is also a personal reflection on spiritually maturing through the stages of life. She writes with disarming candor and clarity, bringing the reader through her own journey while prompting reflection on their own. Donna has touched many lives for God and for good, and I am convinced that this wonderful story will influence and bless many more through the years to come."

—*Joan G. Labarr, retired District Superintendent, North Texas Conference, UMC*

"Laypeople, seminary students and pastors alike will be energized by this refreshingly honest narrative to replace egotism with humble trust in God as the motivation for their ministries. Rev. Donna Whitehead's memoir of ministry, *I Am Enough*, is an invitation to readers to learn from and share in her journey, one we all must make, from faith in our own abilities to faith in God. Donna, one of the first women ordained in the North Texas Conference, UMC, interweaves family memories, insights from her seminary days in the late 1970's, professional lessons learned from her church experiences over the past forty years, and wisdom that has inspired her from authors and mentors."

—*Alyce M. McKenzie, Le Van Professor of Preaching and Worship and Altshuler Distinguished Teaching Professor, Co-Director, The Perkins Center for Preaching Excellence at SMU*

"Clergywomen everywhere, hear these words from Rev. Donna Whitehead, 'I Am Enough!' Throughout history, clergywomen have shared similar stories of doubt. In her memoir, Rev. Whitehead courageously and boldly proclaims, 'I Am Enough!'—three of the most important words a clergy woman can hear. In a real, vulnerable, and humble spirit, Donna helps us join hands as we travel the journey together and proclaim along the way that 'We Are Enough!'"

—*Cynthia Harvey, Bishop, Texas Annual Conference of the United Methodist Church, President of the Council of Bishops, 2022-2024, First Hispanic Woman to lead the Council*

I Am Enough

Rev. Donna Whitehead

Copyright © 2024 by Colinasway Inc.

All rights reserved

Title: I Am Enough
Author: Whitehead, Donna

ISBN: 9798339080176

Publisher: Colinasway Inc.

With gratitude for my grandfather, David Faulkner Edwards, who died the year I was born, passing on to me his passion for life, for learning, and for moving forward

Contents

	Introduction	1
Chapter 1	"Beginning"	7
Chapter 2	"Branching Out"	25
Chapter 3	"Quest"	45
Chapter 4	"Set Apart"	63
Chapter 5	"Preach It"	83
Chapter 6	"End of the Beginning"	99
Chapter 7	"When God Calls"	123
Chapter 8	"Growing Up"	141
Chapter 9	"Facing Difficult Truth"	159

Chapter 10	"Stepping Out"	177
Chapter 11	"Working On It"	199
Chapter 12	"Welcoming Everyone"	217
Chapter 13	"Bringing Light"	241

	Epilogue	261
	Acknowledgements	267
	About the Author	271
	Recommended Reading	273

Introduction

We live our lives going forward, but we understand them by looking backward.
            —Søren Kierkegaard

Let's get real! Getting real is the only way each of us and our churches can have a bright future; each of us must let go of all that keeps us on the surface of life and instead take a deep dive where a genuine connection can be made with God, with each other, and with our Selves (capital S!).

I believe that this cannot be done halfway—it must be all-in. No one left out or uninvited. No one feeling less than or lonely. All are invited to God's table. This is our future: a type of radical intimacy where everyone is respected no matter where a person is on their spiritual journey or what type of church one is involved in.

We need each other, and we need God. God created us to depend on one another. The sooner we discover this, the better.

My hope and prayer is that churches of the future can be a true training ground for a more God-centered way of being church. No more top-down approaches where women or laity or anyone else can be seen as inferior in any way. My part and your part are the same. We all learn from each other, treating each other as equals, listening to the Holy Spirit, and following the radical ways of Jesus. All of us together get real, stay real, live real, and love real. We welcome and become the Real Body of Christ.

So, now the stage is set.

Are you ready to let go of old mindsets that may be limiting your spiritual journey?

Have you ever reached a point when you were restless and felt that there was something more to life—something that you might be missing?

Have you ever thought that your way of looking at God and human beings was no longer working?

Then, keep reading.

My faith journey has been a search for that something more. As I reflected on it, I realized that it has not been so much a journey where I traveled aimlessly from one place to another, as it has been a sojourn where I stopped, became a temporary resident, and then moved on. This has required a deep dive into my soul, and through the twists, turns, obstacles, pride and prejudice, I eventually discovered gold.

Introduction

I discovered along the way—although it took a long time—that God was the main actor in my life. In fact, not until I tried to put on paper a sense of who I am did I really see how much my life was not about me. Yes, it is about the call, the church, my family, how I am wired, strong friendships, and my relationship with others, but like every person's story, it is first and foremost about God showing up again and again. This book includes those times I remember the most.

It's not always been easy. Not at all. And, I imagine this is the case for your journey, too.

I had to awaken to the power of being real and honest before I could acknowledge and face my own weaknesses and vulnerabilities. I had to be humbled before I could move toward all people and learn to "love real." I found that the challenges, highs and lows, celebrations, special moments, and memories along the way were just as important or more important than arriving or reaching the next destination, for I was on a very-focused-at-times quest to discover what it means to be human—to be fully alive.

A similar type of awakening about the church was going on inside of me. As the one place that had always been the center of my life, I had sought meaning inside its walls. My upbringing in a small church in rural northeast Louisiana helped me to enjoy a strong sense of community where everyone mattered and belonged. I took all that for granted.

I Am Enough

In general, church members were alike—white, middle-class, rural, comfortable, and it never occurred to me what might be missing—or better said—*who* might be missing. It was easy to assume that most people were like me.

Pastors came and went in our small-town Methodist congregation, but I respected them and knew they were looked up to—for the most part—in the community. I also loved and respected my parents. They created an environment that was healthy and loving. Everyone was welcomed in our home. No one was criticized or looked down upon.

I remember my mom saying to me early in my life, "You are the one in our family who is driven." I realized that she was right—I wanted to be a leader at school and in youth group; I wanted to make a difference in everything I participated in. I was always looking for depth, for meaning and purpose, for what was good. My sister put it this way: "The details that most people cared about, you were not interested in. And the things you loved the most, few people cared about."

This kind of spiritual seeking led to ordination in 1980. I was the seventh woman ordained in the North Texas Conference of The United Methodist church at a time relatively few women were pursuing such a career. I was blessed to begin my ministry as an associate pastor in a newly formed United Methodist church in a Texas suburb where I

Introduction

spent two wonderful (for the most part) decades. In addition to leading worship, I loved starting new groups, new classes, and new ministries—finding each person's strengths and helping build strong relationships among the congregation. My pioneering spirit (being driven!) matched well with the needs of a young church just getting off the ground and wanting to be known in the community. In the 20 years I was there, the church grew from 240 members in 1980 to 6,700 members in 2000. Today, the congregation of over 4,200 members hosts four worship services on Sunday mornings—8:30 (traditional), 9:45 (modern), 11:00 (traditional), and 12:30 (Spanish).

During my time there, I was on a steep learning curve as I taught, preached, led worship, served others, and helped move the church forward. I grew in my love of scripture, particularly the stories about women facing and overcoming challenges. Outwardly, I was thriving and saw myself as a success. Inwardly, I was catching a glimpse of what it meant to struggle, to stumble, and to not be in control. *Ah, the first step in spiritual growth.*

A major transition occurred when I moved to the second church I was to serve. Soon I discovered that my 1-2-3 plan for church growth would no longer work in this setting—a more established church that was more than 50 years old with a strong sense of identity and a gift I failed to see at first. I was still in my "small s" self, and it took me years to see that instead of changing the church, I was going to have to change myself.

Much to my dismay, information and knowledge were no longer enough. I needed something more. I needed inner strength and a kind of spiritual wisdom that both challenged and humbled me at the same time. I needed to not blame others, to not be a victim. I needed to identify and let go of negative emotions. My soul—along with my heart and mind—needed cultivating. I needed to let go of my old way of pastoring and pay attention to the nudges God was giving me that would lead to growth and flourishing. Most of all, I needed to dwell more in the margins of life where pain and suffering reside. I would have to get real.

This search, this journey, would eventually lead me to God's greatest gift, a gift that awaits your discovery, too!

Donna Whitehead
The Cottage at Hidden Springs, Texas

Chapter One

Beginning

It takes a small town to keep you humble.
—*Bess Streeter Aldrich*

The story of who I am began with the story of one who came before me...

By all accounts, he was a late bloomer—a dreamer in search of purpose and meaning.

As a child, he lived in rural confines and was governed by a city-boy intellect and limitations for all things mechanical: he was no good at farming; he couldn't fix a darn thing.

When cars first appeared in their community, the teen boy, slender and wearing glasses, struggled to learn to drive.

He could not figure out how to maneuver the car through the gate onto the road; instead, he kept going around in circles in the pasture, saying, "I will get it next time!"

On another trip, he had trouble switching gears and drove more than 15 miles to a nearby town in low gear.

"I will get it next time!"

But what a reader of books and newspapers and current events he became.

Aunt Bee would say wistfully, "After working all day in the fields, he stayed up late every night, with a coal oil lamp providing the light, reading into the wee hours of the morning. He was willing to go hungry in order to buy a book. Reading and studying were that important to him."

"He loved to read about history, about different cultures, and about all kinds of people. He was self-taught and never wanted us to sell our textbooks when we were in college because he wanted us to bring them home, so he could read them."

And, what a snappy dresser he was—donning a crisp suit and a colorful bow tie for every important occasion.

Aunt Bee continued, "He delighted in interacting with people throughout the parish and spent every Saturday morning at the courthouse square in the center of Oak Grove, our parish seat, meeting and greeting everyone. He was equally comfortable with farmers, teachers, businesspeople, those who picked cotton, and those who ran gas stations."

Aunt Bee concluded: "He had an incredible zeal for learning. He wanted to learn something new every day. He listened to the radio each morning to keep up on current events. He never held on to the past and always had an eye for the future. He was an optimist who always believed that things could get bigger and better. Oh, he was a people person who was loved by all who knew him."

His name was David.

Kilbourne, Louisiana
Out in the country, the air drips with humidity as I jump into my parents' Pontiac. I am accompanying my mom, Norine, to the Chambliss Grocery Store three miles from where we live in Kilbourne (population: 351). It is a bright, sunny day. I roll down the window and smell the pine trees, along with my favorite flowers—hydrangeas. It is the summer of 1956, and I am ten years old.

Our first stop is my Uncle Herman's Texaco gas station. It is small, but efficient, with two ancient pumps. There is also a block-lettered sign, "Lightsey Lawnmower and Repair Shop," which Uncle Herman runs on the side. He greets me and mentions that my cousin Glynn is helping him in the shop that day. Uncle Herman stands six feet tall and always seems to be in a good mood.

We pass by Majors General Store on the way to the post office. Postmaster Shirley is eager to converse with my mom. Shirley knows everybody in town, as does my mom.

"Did you know that Darlene had her baby?" Shirley asks.

"Yes, isn't that wonderful?" Mom responds.

Shirley continues, "They are coming home tomorrow from the hospital. And the Green boys just left yesterday to go work on the pipeline in south Louisiana."

Mom concludes, "We'll certainly miss them, but they'll return. They have roots here."

Even though the car window is down, I am sweating. Droplets roll down my forehead and trickle down my cheek. It's a typical Louisiana summer.

My hometown is Kilbourne, Louisiana, a great place to grow up. My love for it had to do with family and friends, life experiences, and fond memories. But, what most rural kids inherently love about the country—the woods, the porch sittings, the lore of the animals—somehow escaped me. It was not in my genes. I love Kilbourne to this day, but at age ten, I already knew I was not meant to stay there.

The stately red brick Baptist church stood at attention whenever we drove past it—in contrast to the smaller and almost invisible Pentecostal church. It was the quaint, yet beautiful-to-me, white clapboard Methodist church, however, that we attended each Sunday, that had my heart. I always smiled at the sight of it. It was like a second home to me, a place that my dad's family helped start years before I came along, a place where I had been baptized as an infant, and the faith community where my aunt, uncle, mom, and dad contributed so much.

I was born into that kind of safe and rather simple community. My dad, Wayne, and my mom, Norine, were both high school teachers. An extended family of aunts, uncles, and cousins all lived close by. I felt loved and embraced and known; everyone seemed to be connected or related in some way. I grew up knowing that I mattered and could make a difference in a bigger world out there. It may have helped that I was the first-born, the first daughter, the oldest child. My sister, Diane, was sixteen months younger, and my brother, David, followed six years later.

Aunt Berta and Uncle Buff—my dad's brother and sister-in-law—took care of me when I was young while my mom taught home economics at the local high school. They lived just up the road from our home, on the way to school. I loved staying with them, especially during the Christmas season, when their house looked and smelled like gingerbread. I especially remember the small lighted church Aunt Berta kept on her end table and the interesting "whatnots" scattered throughout her home.

"Hi, Donna!" Aunt Berta would always greet me with warmth. She was a great cook, and I particularly enjoyed the garden vegetables she prepared. I still think of her every time I eat butterbeans and purple-hull peas.

Uncle Buff was a school bus driver and a farmer. He loved animals, particularly cows, which he always named. I remember him feeding the animals, especially the pigs; we called this "slopping the pigs." Once he let me drive the tractor while he tossed corn in the trailer behind me. He was solid, very dependable, and kind. In later years I realized that he was like a father figure for my dad; they were good friends, as well as brothers.

Across the paved road from our home was my dad's sister, Aunt Bee, who was married to Uncle Herman; they had five children. I loved all my aunts, but Aunt Bee had a really big impact on me. I could not wait to hear her stories, for she had an incredible memory and seemed to know something about everything I was interested in.

She knew the details about our family history that no one else remembered, including when all my aunts, uncles, and cousins were born, if they got married, and when most of them died. She was also my fifth-grade teacher and wrote a play that ended up on the local TV stations. I got to be the star in it, and I felt so special; I remember rehearsing for it. Even back then, I loved being the center of attention.

Aunt Bee was also my writing buddy, and I often would go to her and ask, "Can you help me with this assignment?" She was always available, and during my high school years,

Beginning

she helped edit my papers for 4-H Club, Future Homemakers of America projects, English classes, and later my high school graduation speech. She would say, with her pen in hand, "Now, let's see…" and begin to add, delete, or come up with a more descriptive word than I had chosen. She reinforced my love for writing, for correct grammar, for words.

Church was the center of our family's social life. I can't remember a time when going to church and sharing life with the people of God were not deeply important to me. Even as a young child, not much older than a baby, spending time at church was where I felt most at home.

Aunt Bee's role at church was to lead the singing. *Bringing in the sheaves, bringing in the sheaves. We shall come rejoicing, bringing in the sheaves!* I can still hear her clear, strong voice leading the way, year after year—after year. Uncle Buff was just as regular at church. He was the only treasurer I remember the church ever having. He never took a break or rotated with anyone; he gave the monthly finance reports for more than 40 years! My mom was doing more than her part—teaching adult Sunday School every Sunday all those years in addition to teaching school all week. No wonder I grew up thinking every family went to church; it was such a natural part of my life.

It was the indefatigable and tireless Mrs. Thomas—with her hair pulled back in a bun and always wearing a dress—who said the prayer every Sunday. Everyone knew that she did not just talk about God; she *knew* God and was closer to Him than the rest of us. Her prayers showed that. They were longer than most, but no one complained. I learned from her that God was my friend who wanted to help and comfort me and that He speaks. In fact, wonder of wonders, God even wanted to speak to *me*.

I now see that in my younger years, our small Methodist church was already leading the way for women to be strong leaders in the church. My grandmother, along with my grandfather, were charter members. My Great Aunt Carrie started the first Sunday School at the church, and Aunt Bee was certified as a lay speaker in 1963, speaking—or shall I say "preaching"—several times in different churches. No one ever questioned it. I remember hearing her speak on 1 Corinthians 12 once, emphasizing that "there are varieties of gifts, but the same Spirit." It was easy to conclude that the Holy Spirit was not concerned about gender.

Starting School
"Hurry up Donna! We have to be on time for the beginning of school!" I can still hear my dad, Wayne, shouting.

It was so exciting to finally be going to school with my parents, who were both high school teachers. First through twelfth grades were all on one campus, so I never had to worry about a ride to school.

Beginning

Mrs. Sanders was my jovial first-grade teacher. She was short, wore glasses and loved teaching us to read. I delighted in being one of those chosen to read out loud to the second and third graders. I was so proud. I was also learning how to write cursive. Oh, that feeling when I first wrote a capital A, what an accomplishment! And the "B" was next. I had entered a whole new world, a world in which I thrived because I was eager to learn, and school seemed to be the perfect place to do that.

School became my comfort zone; I just loved being there. My need to be first and to be noticed came out in my obsession with getting good grades and being a high achiever—even though I quickly forgot details right after a test, seldom integrating what I had learned into my life. I seemed to need the affirmation that came from being a good student and at the top of the class. I suppose you could say I was ambitious. I liked to dream big dreams about the future but was not very good at getting started or taking the first step.

School and church—these activities consumed my young life.

On Palm Sunday, I walked down the aisle of the Kilbourne Methodist Church to be confirmed at age twelve. I don't remember much about what I did or said, but I do remember how my heart pounded because Brian and Glynn David—who were so handsome and a grade ahead of me—

walked down with me to be confirmed also. I wore my favorite blue church dress, the one my mother had made for me, and I noticed the boys wore ties and had polished their shoes.

"Are you ready?" Glynn David asked.

"I guess so," I shrugged. I hoped he had not figured out that I had a crush on both of them. By then I had discovered that going to church was good, but it was so much better when the boys were there.

While we lived in the country outside a small town, I was not a typical country girl. I did not want to spend time outside doing chores like many of my friends did. I chose to talk, to socialize, to think and discuss ideas and concepts; the chores could wait.

Like my father, I grew up wanting to read, write, and learn. I read all kinds of novels like *Little Women* and *Jane Eyre*, along with mystery books featuring Nancy Drew and Trixie Belden. I tended to study too long and too much for tests. In general, I was an idea person, a social bookworm. I had a very active mind, which could be creative and imaginative—even visionary. This way of relating to the world could be good—especially at school—but the problem was I could easily miss what was going on right in front of me. I remember my mother asking when I entered my teen years, "Donna, why don't you enter this competition?"

"What are the requirements?" I responded.

"You have to identify local plants, trees, and flowers."

"Oh, okay. I can do that," I agreed.

My seventh-grade self was brimming with confidence and blissfully unaware of what I did not know. I had never paid much attention to plants and did not know the difference between an oak leaf and a sweetgum leaf, for starters. I knew hydrangeas but that was about it regarding my floral identification. My mother tried to help, tutoring me on the ten-mile drive to the place where the contest took place, but it was too late. I only got about 20% of the answers right. Why should I have been surprised? I tended to ignore the natural world around me, having my mind on seemingly "more important" things.

Looking back, I'm surprised that doing so poorly in the competition didn't rattle me more, but in truth, I just wasn't interested in plants. My passion was the world of *ideas* and politics and religion and what life was all about. I was already consumed with seeking and searching spiritually, reading a chapter in my Bible every night. Other interests would have to wait.

In addition to teaching school, my parents were active leaders in the community, helping with sporting events and fundraisers for Future Homemakers of America and Future Farmers of America, along with many other worthy causes.

They were available to their students, and my mom reached out to anyone who might need special attention.

Faye McGaha, who was one year older than me and whose face had been scarred in a fire when she was young, came to our home often.

"How is your mom?" my mother would ask Faye.

"She is okay but has been sick a lot lately."

"I will come see her soon," Mom promised.

"That would be wonderful!" Faye's eyes would light up.

Everyone knew that Mom loved Faye, but more importantly, Faye knew it. In fact, Mom loved everyone, it seemed. Years later it hit me that there was never any "us versus them" in our home; Faye, like everyone else, was a friend.

I got my love of sports—particularly basketball—from my dad; he was a natural athlete. My favorite all-time movie is still the 1986 film *Hoosiers* which tells the story of a small-town basketball team and coach in Indiana starting the season out slow but winning the state championship in the end.

"Donna! Take a shot!" my dad shouted.

He was reminding me, along with my sister, Diane, that we could not win the basketball game if we did not attempt a shot in the final moments of a close game, especially when we were behind. He was right, of course. Diane—who was shorter than me, with brown hair and a great jump shot—

played with me for three years on the high school basketball team, the only sport available to girls.

My brother, David, eight years younger than me, also grew up with a strong love of sports. I remember going to his Little League baseball games before I left home, and he always got a hit. In later years he played basketball, and while he was good at scoring, he was even better at the mental part of the game. He was the point guard, the playmaker, and he enjoyed making others look good. He did not have to be the hero himself. I liked that about him then, and I still admire that trait in him today.

Although Diane and I never won the state championship, we have great memories of replaying almost every game with our father. He was a dad first, but he was also a coach, math teacher, and a moral compass. He was available—I see now what a gift that is—and he answered my questions and gave me advice. Best of all, he gave me what every girl needs from her father—his blessing and assurance that I was beautiful in his sight. Even though I wore glasses and was not known for my looks, he told me I was beautiful, and I believed him. When my mother sewed a new dress for me, I always went to my father first for his approval and to ask him how I looked in it. He understood the importance of his role; he affirmed me and gave me the sense of worth and value that every daughter yearns for from her father.

Dad Is My Hero

While my mom was incredibly strong and a wonderful servant, it was my dad who was my hero. Both of them grew up during the Depression and were a part of what Tom Brokaw called "The Greatest Generation." When Dad became restless during World War II, he enlisted and was trained as a pilot in the Army Air Corps. After being shot down over France while flying an A-20 bomber on his 29th mission, he was awarded a Distinguished Flying Cross and a Purple Heart.

It was a memorable day when I discovered the medal as a teenager. "Dad, why have you not mentioned the medal before?" I asked him.

He said simply, "I did not want to dwell on the war, and it did not seem like the right time."

I responded, "But this was important. You showed courage—like so many others—by serving that way. You fought for what you believed in."

He didn't refute the fact but said humbly, "Yes, but it is hard to explain what facing the enemy was really like; it could only be understood by fellow comrades."

I was told that my dad, the fifth of five children, was favored by my grandfather who thought he "hung the moon." But instead of becoming the lawyer my grandfather hoped he would be, Dad returned to his small hometown after the war. At Kilbourne High School, he found his place as a high school coach for boys, a math teacher, and later, after I graduated from high school in 1964, the principal of the school.

I enjoyed asking him about that role, "Dad, what was the hardest part of being a principal?"

He responded, "It was helping the school and community stay calm in a time of change and transition—mid 1960s—when the schools were integrated. I knew integration was the right thing to do and that it was time, so I made a priority out of meeting the new parents, along with the students, and answering questions. I wanted them to feel comfortable and welcomed. There were only a few problems, and we addressed them just like we always had when problems arose."

I still think of him when I drive by small-town high schools throughout the South and wonder what integration was like for their community. My father was a leader, and like my grandfather who had served before him, he found his way to make a difference, especially in a time of change. I now believe his leadership and character influenced me in numerous ways that I'm only just now starting to realize, including my seeking to go into the ministry. At that time—the mid 1960s—and in that place—north Louisiana—racism was such an accepted part of life that my dad's approach to peaceful understanding and integration was quite extraordinary. In an era where we are still wrestling with the scourge of racism, I look back to his example for inspiration and guidance.

Mom Is My Rock

Mom was a risk-taker, the one of nine children who desperately wanted to go to college, the one who cleaned garbage cans as a freshman to make ends meet. She had a zest for life and went for it full force.

If my mother's life had been a movie, the first scene would have been of her picking cotton out in the field shortly after she graduated from high school in Pioneer, Louisiana. Her principal would drive up and tell her dad that she needed to go to college, and that he was there to give her a 25-dollar-a-month scholarship. Her dad thought that girls should just get married, but Mom knew she wanted more.

She went on to graduate with a degree in home economics from Southwestern Louisiana Institute in Lafayette, Louisiana. After becoming a home demonstration agent, marrying my dad, and moving to Kilbourne, she taught home economics to high school girls for 30-plus years. She had goals, and she accomplished them. She plowed new ground.

She had a good marriage with Dad; she also knew how to get things done on her own and could be independent when that was needed. She knew who she was—a beloved child of God. I had always thought of myself as a Daddy's girl, but in

Beginning

my later years my sister surprised me by saying, "You know you got your drive from Mom, don't you? Not from Dad. Mom wanted Dad to be more ambitious."

Why had I never seen that?

Mom had endless energy and tackled community projects of all kinds. She reached out to everyone, helping them to feel included and involved. She didn't just talk about faith; she lived it out in very real and practical ways by serving others.

This was Kilbourne. This was my home. I had everything I needed in that small Louisiana town that loved me so well and nurtured me as a child.

But I couldn't shake a feeling. The world was a big place with so much to explore. I had an itch that needed to be scratched. I wanted, no, I *needed* more.

Chapter Two

Branching Out

The future is not something to predict. The future is something to build.

—*Franco Ongaro*

Teen Years

It's 1960. I am fourteen years old. Christmas is coming, and Dad has an idea. "Let's do something new and different," he says. "Instead of buying a tree, let's find one in the woods near us. After all, there are so many to choose from, and one of them has to be the perfect-shaped tree for us. Let's go look." Off we go on what we consider to be a family adventure.

Dad, however, is not the person to call if you need someone to fix things or put things together. Picking out a tree is one thing; getting it set up is another. After finally selecting the perfect tree, my father and younger brother (who is not mechanical either) somehow wrangle the tree into our house but cannot get it to stand straight or even stand up at all using a Christmas tree stand. When it's finally up, it looks awful. I think to myself, *Why had we chosen that crooked tree?* It's a disaster. After working on it for several hours, everyone agrees that it's time to give up. We will find another way to bond as a family. The next day Dad goes out and purchases a new, pre-cut tree with no assembly required. It is *well* worth the money.

Dad was mechanically challenged, but that wasn't the biggest trial he'd face as our father; it was dealing with the fact that my sister and I liked boys, and much to his dismay, they liked us. He made a rule in our high school years that we could only go out with boys twice a month. At times, we double-dated, and that worked to a certain degree in alleviating his fear of one of us being left alone with someone he did not know well. However, when the new Baptist preacher arrived in town, with a cute son named Mickey who was a junior in high school—the grade between the two of us—each of us, at different times, ended up dating him.

My sister and I were close and talked about our dating life with each other. I remember saying to her, "Diane, Mickey has asked me for a date. Do you mind if I go?"

She responded, "No, that is fine. I am going with Gary now."

"Who is going to ask Dad about this?" I persisted.

Diane said, "You. He will be more likely to say yes to you."

Dad didn't balk at the idea of one of us handing Mickey off to the other. I think he was as amused as we were and was curious to see which one of us would actually end up with him!

Dad survived our dating years, and my high school years went by quickly. Near the end of my senior year, he said in an unusually serious tone that he wanted to talk. He was lighthearted by nature, but this time he had a solemn look on his face. He said, "My role will soon be changing with you. You will be going to college and making more decisions on your own. I won't be around as much."

I responded rather flippantly, "Of course, Dad." My always-look-on-the-bright-side temperament was kicking in, and I made light of what he was saying, but deep down I knew he was right. Life was about to change for me, and I was full of just as much confidence as I was naivety. Dad wouldn't be there to help me distinguish between the two.

I did not like to face unpleasant feelings, so I avoided grieving the ending that was about to occur—no more high school basketball games in the gym I loved, no more social times with my high school friends, no more classes in the school I had been a part of for 12 years. All this was behind me, but I was ready to move on. I was sad, but more than that, I was excited, even eager for what was ahead—a new and much bigger town, new friends, new teachers, new social life, new independence. The anticipation overshadowed everything else. Not to worry, I told myself; letting go and moving on is a good thing.

College Bound
I left home in 1964 and arrived on the Louisiana Tech campus in Ruston, Louisiana, just over 100 miles from home. Ruston was a rather small college town, nestled in the piney woods of northwest Louisiana. It had a kind of charm and an identity centered around the college campus.

However, much that was not charming was going on in our country. There was resistance to civil rights, an escalating conflict in Vietnam, popularity of Elvis and the Beatles, and the Kennedy assassination. As usual, I did not pay much attention to this kind of turmoil; I was busy focusing on my own world—new friends, new teachers, new environment, new classes, and new social life.

Arriving on campus, I was inexperienced and rather naïve, unfamiliar with different ways of thinking and different kinds of people. Things had pretty much gone the way I wanted them to all my young life. I remember being very upset once because I thought we might move in the eighth grade when Dad got a new job opportunity and how relieved I was when he did not take it. Again, I avoided having to really struggle, to experience emotional pain, to adapt, or to make new friends. I spent much of my time reading books, but they were mainly about people who were like me. I ventured out to larger cities occasionally, but never stayed there long enough to understand a different kind of culture. My world remained fairly small and limited.

As a by-product of this small world, I developed certain biases; I later called them blind spots. I was biased toward education and people who loved it like I did; that was the world I was comfortable in. Since my father's family seemed to be populated by teachers and educators, it appeared to me to be "better than" my mom's family, full of salespeople, truck drivers, artists, even alcoholics. Oh dear! With eight siblings, her family was rather messy and complicated; someone was always getting married, or divorced, or facing some type of crisis. Couldn't they get their lives together and quit making all these mistakes?

I did not know much about myself and how I related to the world. I had not yet seen that my tendency was to avoid anything painful or unsettling. I wanted the world to be a positive and good place all the time and assumed everyone thought like that.

It would take me years to see how sheltered I was growing up. There were no minor or major crises in my life, little real struggle or tension, and little fighting or conflict in my home. While this lack of conflict was a good thing, it did not particularly prepare me for the kind of decisions that I needed to make as I entered a world that was changing on several fronts.

Needless to say, growing pains were about to hit me hard. In the early summer of 1964, I was making the transition from being a big fish in a little pond—being at the top of my class and daughter of the principal—to an environment where none of that mattered, and I knew no one.

But true to my nature, I looked forward to the challenge. Being overconfident was definitely one of my personality traits!

I decided to major in secondary education—probably because I had come from a long line of teachers. I was also close to my high school English teacher and chose English as my first teaching field and then decided on math as my second field. Again, I was influenced by my father who had taught high school algebra and geometry.

I expected to soar academically at Louisiana Tech just as I had in high school. Soon, however, I was struggling to pass biology pop quizzes, and my math classes proved to be way over my head. I was catching a glimpse of how little I knew in some areas. The good news is that I was humble and wise enough to get help when I needed it, and an important seed was planted. Depending on others is a strength—not a weakness.

I made a good social decision by agreeing to be the athletic director for our dorm, representing it in every kind of athletic event. This position turned out to be a wonderful way to make new friends, and I was beginning to feel like I belonged in this new college community. Not everything went smoothly at school, however. I returned to my dorm room one Friday night from the campus library to learn that I had been grounded (required to stay on campus the next weekend) because I had missed my 8:00 p.m. curfew. This goody-two-shoes girl who always did the right thing had been caught staying out too late—studying in the library of all places! I wasn't even on a date. It made a big impression on me. I had broken the rules, and I was being punished. I did not want to do that again—even if the library beckoned.

In general, my social life was picking up; I was dating a young man named Don. I met him in the cafeteria line near the beginning of the fall semester. He was a senior. I was a freshman.

"So, you are from Lake Providence?" I asked.

"Yes, I know Kilbourne, your hometown, well."

"I have been to Lake Providence on several occasions. The lake there is beautiful."

Don and I had a common bond, and we were off and running. From the beginning I was drawn to his confidence, clean-cut, blond, handsome look, love of football and sports, age (five years older), and intellect and steadiness as an engineering student. I admired the fact that he had worked all during his high school years, and in many ways was a self-made man. He was someone whom I could depend on. I also loved his 1958 Chevrolet Impala—even if he drove it too fast, and on one of our first dates, he did not make a turn and instead crashed into a tree. We were fine, but it shook me up enough that I was excused from taking a big math exam the next day. Lucky me!

Two Become One
I fell in love, and love swept me into a new life, in retrospect, in a flash. My college life as a single woman ended when I took the fall semester off in 1965 to marry Don. The year before—during his senior year—he interviewed for jobs.

"So how did your job interview go?" I asked.

He responded, "It went well. I am seriously considering the job at Texas Instruments in Dallas."

Excitedly I said, "I think Dallas would be a great place to live!" And it was. We used the remainder of Don's paycheck to secure our first apartment in northwest Dallas, and I continued my studies in January in Denton, Texas, at what is now known as the University of North Texas.

When I look back on this time in my life—I had just turned 19—I realize I did not reflect on much of anything, including getting married. I knew that I was in love and wanted to be with Don. It was that simple. Never mind that his family life had been very bumpy and difficult growing up. Love would take care of that.

What happened to the idea that I was going to have to change, grow up, and find my own way? Maybe that could wait. The good news was that Don was mature and stable with a job. So, off we went. I saw Don as a protector, a problem-solver, and a fixer of anything broken; he had the life experience I was lacking, and I am sure I thought he could keep my life stable and secure like my parents had always done. After all, isn't security and stability what is most important?

I think Don was drawn to my high energy and love of people. If he had any doubts about getting married, or about anything, he didn't express them. Instead, he gave the impression that he knew just about everything—like a good engineer. I happily followed his lead.

We went through a honeymoon period, but like most honeymoons, it did not last for long. In my junior year of college, I learned in a psychology class the importance of family backgrounds in forming who we are as adults. It was dawning on me that Don and I had vastly different family experiences and personalities. We started most conversations from two different places. I might say, "Let's give a regular gift to the church."

Don would say, "There is no room in our budget for that."
I would retort, "Could we talk about it?"
He would emphatically respond, "No, first things first!"
Don left little room for doubt and questioning.

Like many marriages, we were drawn to traits in each other we did not see in ourselves—which was great in the falling-in-love stage, but not so great when we had to face our differences. I was intuitive and idealistic while he was very practical, comfortable in the technical and mechanical world. I tended to be over the top and talked a lot; Don was more cautious, reserved, and uncomfortable verbalizing feelings. I was an extrovert and wanted to have people around often; he was an introvert and was content—even thrived—when alone. Because of his family background, he had made a decision never to depend on other people—including me— while I tended to be overly dependent on others, including him. We needed each other and had much to learn from one another—if we were open to it.

I was coming to the unsettling conclusion that I could not change Don; I could only change myself. I caught a glimpse—just a glimpse—of the truth that I had some traits that needed to be changed. Could I be part of the problem?

I learned through these trials to really commit to working through friction in the relationship instead of maintaining a carefree attitude about everything. I also learned to choose my battles and to yield at times because most of the things we disagreed about were not that important.

My undergraduate degree was finished in two and a half years; I thrived in my English classes—lots of words, ideas, stories, reading, and writing. However, I was humbled by a calculus class in my second year. You could say that it ate my lunch. That semester, I made five As and one D. I was beginning to get it. I was really good in some subjects and terrible in others. There didn't seem to be much in between.

My student teaching in Dallas was completed at Cary Jr. High. I then got a job there teaching eighth-grade math and algebra because that was where the opening was. (I did not teach calculus.) The school environment felt comfortable to me, but I worked under a burned-out supervisor who saw teaching as a job she had to finish so she could retire. I made a mental note that I always wanted to have passion for my work and continue to develop new interests as I grew older.

Young and Restless

Don and I were entering the world of things we could not control despite our best plans. A bump in the road occurred when we decided we were ready to have our first child.

"We have been married long enough, and you are almost 29. Why don't we try to have a baby?" I asked.

"Yes, I am fine with that," Don replied.

"Good. I am going to stop teaching, so that we can start our family."

I struggled to get pregnant but eventually found a gynecologist who was a fertility expert, and in 1970, five years after we married, I became pregnant with our daughter, Wendi. Yes!

However, instead of being happy that my dream had come true, something shifted emotionally, and I began to lose my zest for life. I felt down, depressed, probably related to hormones during my pregnancy. Where had the positive, optimistic Donna gone? I couldn't find her. And I did not know what to do about it. Until then, my identity had been centered around my role as a student and a teacher. I had quit teaching, and there seemed to be nothing to replace the confidence I had gained from working.

Something was out of kilter.

We had purchased a home, and I was trying my best to be a good homemaker like my mom and aunt. I even bought a new sewing machine, a clear sign that I did not know myself at all. I was terrible at both cooking and sewing, making me feel more insecure than ever. Who was I apart from a daughter, a mother, a wife, and a not very good homemaker? I had no idea.

In an effort to regain my equilibrium during the pregnancy, I returned for a brief time to my parents' home in northeast Louisiana, hoping to rediscover there what was missing in my life. It was difficult to explain to my friends why I had come home. How did I tell these people I loved that something was wrong? How could I say that I was lost when everyone around me seemed to be found? How could I tell others that I didn't know who I was and felt empty inside? Why wasn't the fact that I was pregnant enough to make me happy and content?

I was searching for that feeling of feeling okay again, and the last time I felt that was at home. But after being there a little while, it was clear that being around my parents again wasn't the cure I'd hoped it would be. They were nice about it, but the truth is that hormones during pregnancy can be very powerful. Women often go through depression before or after the birth of their baby, and that's exactly what I was experiencing. There was nothing my parents or my hometown could have done about it.

Thankfully, things got better when our daughter, Wendi, arrived. The entire birth experience, which was a type of miracle, seemed too good to be true. I was thrilled to have a daughter—and a healthy one at that. Her birth—and all the hopes and dreams for the future that she represented—thrust me out of putting the focus on myself. Life was becoming an adventure again, and I had a daughter and husband who needed me. It was enough—more than enough.

It was March 1971, and like our country, I had made it through the '60s. It had been seven years since I graduated from high school, and in those years, this Louisiana-turned-Texas girl had married, finished college, taught school, and now had her first child—all by the age of 25. I was on the path to becoming a good wife and mom, and I convinced myself I was not that different from my friends who all seemed to be content to be homemakers and raise their children.

I found a way to be busy with all kinds of mom activities, and I began to feel like my old self. I had meaning and purpose again. However, I did not try to sew. (I had never once used the sewing machine). The next time my mom came to visit; I gave the machine to her! As I look back, it was my first real acknowledgment that I did not have to be like others or become what they might expect me to be. Maybe—just maybe—it was enough to be myself. Could I trust the uniqueness that God had given me?

The lesson of letting go, which I began to learn when I graduated from high school, came flooding back. It was now time to let go of a need to be like others, so that a truer way of being myself could come forth. Three years later, in March 1974, at age 27, when I was four months pregnant with Trey—our second child—that future began to unfold. Not only was I about to give birth to a son; I was also preparing to birth a newer, more mature version of *me*.

An Epiphany—Truth
The restlessness had come back. That weird feeling in the pit of my stomach would not go away, and standing by the window in the kitchen of our home in Plano, I experienced a moment of inspiration and truth. It became crystal clear to me that I needed to take more responsibility for my own life—to become more self-defined. As much as he might

want to, Don could not be responsible for my happiness, just as I could not do that for him.

We were good together, but I had defined my path by his path. He was five years my senior, he had a solid engineering mind, and he could provide a confident answer to just about every question. It was easy just to follow him, but I knew it was time for me to grow up and stop trying to live out my life dreams and hopes solely through him.

The other problem we were having was money. Don's experience growing up had caused him to find his security in money, so he resorted to controlling the budget as tightly as he could. This left little room for spending money on anything other than what was absolutely necessary. This was affecting us both, and there didn't seem to be enough breathing room in our relationship.

Standing there in the kitchen by the window with all of these thoughts swirling around in my head, I realized it was time for me to make a change. The Holy Spirit was speaking.

I remembered a conversation a few days earlier with Don when I said, "Your colleague, Bill, just got a great promotion. Wonder if you will get one?"

He responded, without looking up, "Probably not. That's not important to me."

I said, "Don't you want to move up in your field and be recognized for your expertise and strengths?"

He responded, "I hate politics; I have no intention of pleasing others to move up the ladder."

Oh dear! He was happy the way he was.

I was the one who was unhappy with the status quo. It was my problem, my restlessness. I could not change Don, but I could change myself. It felt uncomfortable, unsettling, even scary and uneasy to face this truth. This moment was life-changing, and the awareness first made me sad, like something was dying inside of me—maybe the dream of a perfect marriage, the hope for an easy life with little struggling or pain, the desire to have everything go my way.

I knew, however, there would be much more to come in our story, and I was right. In the future, Don supported me in my desire for a deeper purpose and a way to serve the broader community. He understood that I was restless and needed a different kind of challenge. We also knew that we could continue to be partners as we moved forward; our love could get stronger.

Shortly after this awakening, it was no accident or coincidence that my friend, Sharon, asked me if I wanted to join her in pursuing a Master of Liberal Arts at Southern Methodist University. I immediately said *yes!* This meant more school, more learning. The plan was that we would commute to night classes together while our husbands kept the children. Don agreed, and Sharon and I moved forward by enrolling.

Branching Out

I was so ready for this new intellectual challenge. All the courses were good, but there was one that was particularly appealing to me. It was called *The Human Condition* and taught by a rabbi I had heard of—Rabbi Levi Olan.

Born in Ukraine in 1903 and raised in New York, Rabbi Olan rose to national prominence as a leader in Reform Judaism, moving to Dallas in 1948 to shepherd the largest Jewish congregation in the South at Temple Emanu-El. He may have been advanced in years when I first took his class at SMU, but no one could mistake him for being stuffy or out of touch! It was right here in conservative Texas that he became a leading voice of progressive views on civil rights, poverty, war, and everything else. The local WFAA radio station gave him a half-hour show on Sunday mornings that reached upwards of 200,000 listeners who tuned in to hear him muse on issues as global as the Vietnam War and as locally relevant as the assassination of John F. Kennedy. Whether you agreed or disagreed with Rabbi Olan, his care for people and his highly respected opinions earned him the title, "The Conscience of Dallas."

As an advocate of school desegregation—like my father—Rabbi Olan had the respect of civil rights leaders in Dallas. His home was vandalized, he received hate mail, and his synagogue received a bomb threat just because he took a stand for peaceful integration in 1954 when Dallas had defied the Supreme Court's decision in *Brown v. Board*. It's no wonder that he was frequently asked to deliver sermons at local churches and was teaching at a Methodist university. There I was, taking a class from The Conscience of Dallas!

I hung on every word he said. I knew he had the kind of spiritual wisdom I was hungry for. When students were asked to write a paper summarizing what they had learned at the end of his class, I was ready. I spent a couple of days going through all my notes from class, and as I wrote, I had a moment—another break-through moment. Into my small-town, now-suburban, white, middle-class, rather fixed Christian world view came a word from God that I desperately needed, an insight I'd been searching for: "Truth is found in paradox."

Epiphany!

This insight blew my mind; it was so freeing to me. In the world of absolutes, right and wrongs, yeses and noes, I had discovered another way—the unexpected treasure of the in-betweens. It felt like a door had opened, that my brain had expanded, that a new world beckoned me. I no longer felt boxed in or limited by either/or ways of thinking.

It had been bothering me that I thought I had to choose between my Christian faith and what I was learning in my college courses. I could now put the two worlds together. And in my faith journey, the paradox that Jesus was both fully human and fully divine—both at the same time—was beginning to make sense. These two different truths could co-exist, side by side.

Even more important, I was catching a glimpse—if only for a moment—of how much I needed to hear from not just those who thought like I did, but from those who saw things differently. I did not have to have all the answers; I could listen and connect with anyone anywhere—in their humanity—without worrying about losing the truth I was searching for. Oprah Winfrey would later call these kinds of breakthroughs "aha" moments, when something hits people as SO true that they never see life the same way again. It was that kind of moment, stirring hope and excitement inside of me. For the first time in a long time, I felt very alive.

Paul had his revelation on the road to Damascus, and I was having mine—maybe not as dramatic, but certainly as life-changing. Interestingly, it did not come from inside a church, but from a Jewish rabbi in a college classroom. Evidently, God speaks when and wherever people are restless enough to hear Him. This revelation connected me with my soul, taking away much of my confusion and angst. I knew I desperately wanted and needed more soul moments like this. And, I knew I could embark on a journey that would forever leave me changed. The search was on.

Chapter Three

Quest

When the opposites are realized to be one, discord melts into harmony, battles become dances, and old enemies become lovers. We are then in a position to make friends with all of our universe, not just half of it.

—Ken Wilbur

Discovering Kindred Spirits

At the age of 28, I was in a full-blown search for who I was, who Jesus was, and what the truth was. The shift I experienced in Rabbi Olan's class proved to be the first step that I needed. I felt alone in this quest at first, finding few others I could talk to. It was not the kind of casual conversation that I could have with most of the people in my life. However, I knew I was tuned in and would eventually find some others like me. That is exactly what happened.

Since I tended to be a thinker and had always been very curious about spiritual matters, I knew that this kind of hunger was more than curiosity. I had questions—lots and lots of questions—and I began to look for people I could connect with who would understand, who were wise and mature. I made a list of the five people around me whom I most admired, and to my surprise, three of them were United Methodist pastors. A pattern was emerging. What was God saying?

At the top of my list was Rev. Bourdon Smith, the pastor of the small United Methodist church where Don and I had been attending. To me, he was the United Methodist version of Rabbi Olan—wise in a down-home way, steeped in scripture, and well-grounded in the biblical view of the world. I knew he was someone I could learn from.

He was an engaging preacher and told Bible stories so well that I listened intently to everything he said. He opened the scriptures for me in a way that was exciting and fresh; I had no idea these stories—these ancient parables—could be so powerful and relevant. Rev. Smith—it seemed natural to call him Bourdon—was also interesting to me as a person. I invited him over to our home for a meal—a big step for me since I was not into cooking or preparing meals. I wanted to know about his life, his faith, his journey into ministry.

In fact, I wanted to know his perspective on just about everything. I asked Bourdon, "How did you decide to go into the ministry?"

He replied, "I knew from a fairly early age that I wanted to be a pastor and preacher. I had a pastor friend who encouraged me."

I continued, "You seem comfortable with being honest about yourself and your flaws. You come across as very human. Do you feel pressure to act like a preacher?"

He smiled and replied, "No, I really don't. I believe that God does not want us to take ourselves too seriously."

He seemed comfortable being both human *and* holy. What a relief. In the next few months and years, I was blessed to find a few others—including two women—who had this kind of passion about spiritual matters and who were beginning to think about attending seminary. I no longer felt alone.

It was not, however, until I discovered the biography of Mary Fletcher—one of the female leaders of early Methodism—that I was able to connect with women from another era and see that I certainly was not the first woman to feel this deep calling to know more about God. She was born in 1739 in England, but her story was not published until 1997. When I finally read it, I felt like I had found a soulmate.

Her friends described Mary as an enthusiast. I love that word. It was used to describe her because she went around asking spiritual questions of anyone who could help her in her desire to find "a deeper religion than she had known." I was so relieved and excited to find a kindred spirit like her—from the 1700s, no less.

After finding a group of women—she called them "lively souls"—among the Methodists, Fletcher went on to become a key part of the Methodist movement with a clear call to serve others. When the "woman question" was broached with John Wesley, the founder of The Methodist Church, he wisely said that she had an "extraordinary call" that was an exception to the ordinary rules they operated under. He was practical enough to know that he needed souls on fire like hers to help with the movement sweeping England, and he found a way to affirm her as an equal to men.

Good move, John.

I realized that I could be an "enthusiast" like Mary Fletcher, and I could continue to look for others who were lively souls searching for a deeper faith. With guidance from mentors along the way, I was discovering how inspiring scripture could be, and I realized that the joys and struggles of biblical heroes like Paul and Mary Magdalene were like mine today. The connection was made; everyone is alike, including the people in the Bible, because all are human beings on some sort of quest about what it means to be a human being in relationship to God.

This desire—almost obsession—for more learning gave me the confidence to ask for a catalog of courses offered at Perkins School of Theology, the United Methodist seminary in Dallas, which was close to my home. I opened the catalog and could not put it down. I wanted to take every class. It seemed too good to be true that I had found a place this stimulating, and I longed to be a part of a community where questions about God were being discussed and talked about—a place where other people were hungry for spiritual knowledge. While I had no idea what I would do when I finished the courses, I knew I had to pursue this.

When I came back to earth, I realized there were several issues to deal with. My family and my friends were not particularly excited about my new possibilities. One of my friends asked, "What is wrong with you? Are you having a mid-life crisis?"

My mom—who had been a full-time teacher all my life as well as an attentive and giving mother—kept saying to me, "What about the children? Are you sure you want to do this?"

This was an interesting question from a woman who had leaned in and flourished with a beyond-busy life. She had worked full-time herself, taught an adult Sunday School class for more than 40 years with near-perfect attendance, and had been an incredible mom to Diane, David, and me. In fact, I

I Am Enough

never remember asking anything from her that she did not give me. She was that available to us.

As a woman, she was powerful, but—in hindsight—not in the way people tend to value. It was a kind of inner strength, the much-needed trait of resilience and flourishing despite limitations. She had this trait in spades and showed that characteristic often, especially in the last ten years of her life when she had dementia. She never gave up helping others and doing more than her part in every activity. Clearly I was inspired by her.

And then there was the church itself. It was 1977; the church was—and still is—the most conservative institution in the country. There were very few women enrolled in seminary. There were no female preachers in churches that I knew of and no clear professional path for the few who did graduate from seminary. I would be entering a male-dominated world and going up against a strong, patriarchal system with ancient traditions. Did I know what I was getting into?

I just knew that I was not going to let those things get in my way because I had the support from the one who mattered the most, my husband Don. In many ways, he was the most supportive of all, and he encouraged me and came through financially to support my pursuit—yet again. He also reminded me that this journey was about me, not him. I remember him saying, "Okay, but do not expect me to change or to become more spiritual."

I knew exactly what he meant. Don grew up in the church and had a respect for all that is holy, but he was not wired spiritually the way I was. He was very practical. It made him a good engineer, but he would never be the cookie-cutter spouse of a church pastor. My pursuit of the spiritual rubbing against his mind for the practical could have been a source of serious friction between us, but I believe that the terms he laid out between us from the start made our marriage work, while so many others around us didn't survive. Many of my women friends who chose to go to seminary at that time ended up getting divorced. When Don and I agreed that we had two different things going for us and that self-definition was okay—even good—we thrived when we were together.

I had the good sense to appreciate Don's continued support, for it was a big decision that would change our family life in the years to come. I promised him that seminary would be a sound investment because it was an investment in *me*. It took me years to see some of the sacrifices that Don has made. By then my driven side had kicked in, and I was focused on pushing forward, determined to keep learning.

I did struggle when I first left our three-year-old son, Trey, in a nursery at Perkins School of Theology. He did not like it, and I didn't either. So, I came home and asked my neighbor—who had a son near his age—to take care of him when I was in class. That arrangement worked, but I still felt sad each time I dropped him off.

I realized that I was not particularly good at being a traditional homemaker; my gifts were just not there. I attended most of the PTA meetings in our children's school, and I never missed any of their sporting events. I learned that families were like mobiles, and that when one member of the family makes a move or shakes up the status quo, everyone in the family must adapt to regain stability. I was grateful that we thrived as a family—for the most part—despite my nontraditional path.

We certainly did not become a perfect two-parent family with a daughter and a son. I had to grow up with the children, learning who I was and what I was called to do with my life. Don was growing too, learning how to heal from his painful family history. We were learning to love each other by forgiving each other and ourselves, learning how to fight and disagree without hurting one another.

I also discovered how important my role as a mother was. More than anything, I wanted Wendi and Trey to have good self-esteem, and I wanted to do everything I could to boost it. I loved affirming, encouraging, and even blessing them. I wanted them to know how special they were—not just on the outside, but on the inside where it mattered even more. I did not want them to struggle or feel the emptiness I had experienced as an adult, wrestling with my identity and self-esteem. I wanted them to know they could be anything they wanted; the sky was the limit. Slowly, I was beginning to believe this truth about myself.

Seminary Bound

It was 1977. I was 31 years old, and I had made a decision that was to have lifelong implications. I was a part of the second wave of women who entered Perkins School of Theology that year. I felt like a pioneer on what was not exactly a battlefield, but it was a place where I would need to forge a new path with the possibility of many bumps in the road.

In many ways it was good for me—a place where I could not only be around people I found stimulating, but a safe place where I could work on the issue of who I was, who God was, and what my relationship with God could be like.

One day I ran into one of my favorite professors as I walked across campus. He asked, "How are things going?"

I replied, "I love it here so much. I don't ever want to leave this place!"

He said, "Glad you like it, but don't get too comfortable. You are being prepared to go out into the world, as John Wesley said."

Umm… Guess I couldn't be a student forever.

I loved seminary life like I loved school earlier in my life. I had found companions—soul searchers, women and men who were asking questions like the ones I was asking. I was delighted that people in this setting did not tell me that my head was in the clouds or that I had to be more practical. They did not say I had to learn to cook or sew to be a good wife and mother. They did not tell me that I needed to be certain about what I believed.

Instead, they encouraged me to ask the questions that I had inside of me, including the ones that I was just beginning to verbalize, like, "Can doubt and strong faith go together?" and "Who is this God people speak of so easily?" I was finding the rich community and depth of inquiry I yearned for, a place where no question was off-limits. It felt like it was a home away from home.

This was such a strong contrast to some of the teaching I had listened to before seminary.

Top-Down Hierarchy

In the early 1970s (when I was in my mid 20s), I attended a seminar given by Bill Gothard, a minister who was well-known for his conservative and traditional teachings. Thousands of women and men flocked to these sessions, particularly in the southern Bible Belt. I was one of them. I knew something was missing in my life, so I went looking for answers, for certainty, and for a spiritual place to land. I found it, temporarily, in Bill Gothard's course entitled Basic Life Principles.

Those looking for matter-of-fact teaching about how to orient their lives and lead their families found a refuge in Gothard's seminars, which included Baby Boomers, as well as pastors and even prominent political leaders. He taught his "basic life principles" as universal truths that everyone should follow if they wanted their families to thrive. If you didn't follow his teachings, he suggested that your life could be in moral jeopardy.

The main thing I remember from his teaching was his strong sense of confidence in his principles of authority. His way of looking at the world and the human condition was hierarchal and top-down; he believed that God—in an effort to protect and bring order to the world—had declared that the male was always to be at the top of the chain of command. Women were expected to obey men in every way—in marriage, the workplace, and the church. It was called the "Umbrella of Authority," and it was memorably illustrated with three umbrellas—the largest one at the top symbolizing Christ, a smaller one below symbolizing the husband, and the smallest below that, symbolizing the wife who keeps the children under her protective care. Gothard believed and taught that these principles came straight from scripture; he did not acknowledge that it was his interpretation of scripture that led him to this conclusion.

It may be hard to believe that Gothard's teachings were ever that popular, especially since they've fallen out of favor today due to many criticisms from Christian leaders and due to Gothard's fall from grace because of his own personal life choices. He eventually stepped down from his role at the Institute of Basic Life Principles in 2014 after dozens of women came forward with accusations that he had sexually harassed them.

Of course, none of this was known when I took his seminar. I listened to him and tried to make sense of his beliefs. I wanted to be a good Christian, and I heard Gothard saying that my part was to follow the men in my life—no need to think for myself.

It was no accident that about a year or so after the Bill Gothard seminar I had the life-transforming experience at my kitchen window, an epiphany where I believe that God spoke to me, telling me to take responsibility for my own life.

This voice encouraged me to move forward by walking alongside the men in my life, listening and working through issues *with* them, instead of always submitting myself "under their authority." This insight called for a loss of innocence, a loss of simplicity, but along with that loss came a tremendous gain, a new kind of wisdom and maturity. I realized that often God doesn't speak in a loud voice, but He can speak clearly yet gently in a way we can hear and understand. I also realized that the insight I received was profound and deep enough that I knew it came from someplace other than me. Welcome, Holy Spirit!

That breakthrough moment, along with the Rabbi Olan insight that truth is found in paradox, gave me the wisdom to move out of the either/or world into the yes/and world. I could focus on my own growth *and* be a good wife and mother. I could respond *and* initiate. I could be gentle *and* strong. I did not have to choose between the two worlds!

That was partly why I felt such a sense of euphoria about being a part of the Perkins community. All was not easy, however. With the sense of euphoria also came a feeling of being overwhelmed with my biblical and theological classes. Just like my first classes in college, everyone else seemed more prepared than I was, and I was constantly trying to keep up. While most students had read the entire Bible at least once, my early years at home of reading a chapter every night—with no context or understanding—were not helping at all. I had to work at not being intimidated or afraid.

I did know I wanted to learn more about God and figure some things out. I got more than I bargained for. In that first semester I naively signed up for an *Introduction to Theology* class taught by Rev. Dr. Schubert Ogden, who had a reputation for challenging his students with tough questions. After the first class, I was terrified he might call on me. It took courage to go to class, and I soon hired a tutor to help me learn what I considered to be an entirely new language. With a lot of prayer, I eventually found my stride and began to enjoy the reading and writing—tons of it. It was my world, after all. Could I relax and learn to lean into it?

During my third year at Perkins, I was asked to write an article for a Perkins newsletter about "Juggling Home and School." My lifestyle was seen as a remarkable feat back then, and on some days, it did feel like I was living in two different worlds. I thought back to the strong female role models in my family and how they had juggled their schedules and had never made a big deal out of it. My mother and grandmother never believed that women were to stay in their place—or in fact, just one place.

Women had come before me who had gotten little attention but who had blazed similar trails. What made my story somewhat unique is that I was a suburban housewife with young children in the midst of academically motivated women pursuing a calling in a very male-dominated field. I found the juggling image a helpful one.

I also was growing spiritually, realizing that most things I had once thought of as coincidence or good luck had been much more than that. God had always been right in the middle of it all, in ways that I did not fully understand yet. The journey was not as centered on me as I once thought.

The changes and adjustments that I was making personally were also going on in the Perkins community. The women students were there for various reasons. Some, like me, came to learn and explore their faith; others had been called to serve the church. Some came to be trained as chaplains or counselors or some other role outside the church. At any rate, women were clearly a minority in all of those categories. There were only one or two other women in my classes, and we tended to gravitate toward each other.

Many of the students, both men and women, were questioning whether it was consistent with scripture for women to lead and preach. Since I was new on the scene, I took a low profile and was not ready to defend my right to preach or be in seminary. I just wanted to listen and learn, be a student, and blend in. However, over the next few years I did find quite a bit of ammunition in Scripture for women needing to step up to the plate along with men in the church—especially when they were called to do so.

And whether I wanted to or not, it was a time to deal with women's issues. I was soon introduced to one of the most hot-button ones—inclusive language, or using female pronouns, along with male ones, for persons and, at times, for God. Since I did not like conflict, I resisted the need for that kind of change. Why were people making a big deal out of something that might not be that important? The issue seemed to bring out strong opinions, and I did not know where I stood. I wanted to understand both sides.

One of my women friends commented, "I don't see any reason to stop using the word 'man' to refer to all people. That term is understood by everyone, and people don't need to change what has worked just fine all these years."

I replied, "Yes, it can be awkward and feel strange at first, but perhaps women have underestimated the power of language to define and shape how they see themselves as women."

She persisted, "It seems equally unnecessary to refer to God as anything other than Father. That term is familiar and personal and good enough for me. After all, Jesus called God Father more than other references."

I countered, "That's a good point. It does seem, however, that Jesus also talked about God as Spirit and Light and Love."

Over time I became convinced that language in general, and inclusive language in particular, is important—very important. I realized it is a factor in helping women in the local church and in our society in general to value themselves more, to see themselves in new roles. I noticed that women entering seminary after me seemed to have healthier self-esteem and greater clarity about their calls to ministry, and it made sense that this progress was partly helped by bringing female pronouns into our speech. As I look back, I am grateful that I was right in the middle of a battle worth fighting and that my four granddaughters have good self-esteem today, feeling few limitations about what they can do—regardless of their gender.

Another power shift happened in seminary as more women moved into classes that had traditionally been dominated by men. While most people in the community would say that the presence of women was a good thing, our being there did seem to bring out unresolved power dynamics between the two sexes.

Every woman I knew in seminary had been mentored by a male who believed in them and helped them identify their calling, and many men were instrumental in leading the way to make room for women. As women stepped up, however, some men—usually in positions of power—struggled with acknowledging that the ways they had related to women for years were no longer going to work or be accepted. Women were struggling too, trying to define their new roles with men. It was a time of change for both sexes, a learning curve for everyone.

All this came to the forefront when the roots of the "Me Too" movement were planted (for me) in the late 1970s at Perkins when one of my clergywomen friends published a paper entitled, "Everything You Ever Wanted to Know About Women's Experiences … But Were Afraid to Ask." It told the story of 20 women students who had been sexually harassed in one way or another in the Perkins community or in a church community—another reminder that changes in language, self-awareness, relationships, and attitudes were long overdue.

I Am Enough

All of this was very troubling to me on several different levels. As I thought back on my top-down hierarchal days with Bill Gothard (still not knowing the allegations of sexual harassment that would be brought against him many years later) and all that his worldview implied, it appeared that fear of change and the need to control was a driving force behind much of this kind of thinking. It seemed that fear of Muslims was replacing the fear of 1950s communists, along with a long list of other groups that were frequently attacked on opinion pages in American newspapers—feminists, liberals, secular humanists, homosexuals, governments, United Nations, and immigrants.

This was the cultural, political, and religious stewpot into which I was about to become another ingredient. I did wonder at times what I had gotten myself into.

Chapter Four

Set Apart

The problem with spending your life climbing up the ladder is that you will go right past Jesus, for he's coming down.

—John Ortberg

Am I Called?
The '70s were coming to a close, and so was my full-time career as a seminarian. I did not want to think about leaving this incubator for body, mind, and soul, but my promise to Don had a practical aspect: I needed to prepare myself for a job.

In 1979 I was selected to be an intern for one year at Highland Park United Methodist Church, the large and impressive church on the edge of the Perkins campus, in the heart of north Dallas. It was a wonderful church with seasoned staff, and it provided the perfect place for me to explore my next steps. Even though I did not know it at the time, this opportunity gave me a strong jumpstart and set the tone for my next 40-plus years in ministry.

I was not sure I was ready for Highland Park. In my early years I had been a part of a very small Methodist church with around 50 members; Highland Park had 5,000. I had no pastors or mentors in my family history and had never seen a woman preach, except for my preaching class at Perkins. I would be the first woman to be an intern at Highland Park, following several successful men.

In my hometown, pastors had come and gone every few years. I had never been especially close to any of them. I had been a leader in high school and college, but Highland Park was quite a different kind of playing field. I knew it was unique—a wonderful training ground with several experienced pastors—and I did not want to blow my opportunity.

I ended up having a wonderful supervisor, Rev. Floyd Patterson, who was a father figure to me. From the first day I met him, I knew he would be exactly what I needed. "Welcome, Donna!" he said. "I want to be sure that you get to experience every ministry in the church—from preschool and nursery to all ages of adults, from discipleship to missions, from finance and stewardship to evangelism." He acted as if it was no big deal that I was a woman, and he gave me a set of Barclay commentaries to celebrate my entry into preaching. I was in the mix and on the team.

A big decision was looming on the horizon, however. Was I going to stay as a student and move into a specialized ministry, or was I called to the local church? The year before my internship, I had begun the process for ordained ministry in The United Methodist Church North Texas Conference. It was a big leap, and I stalled—not ready to declare before this very official group that I knew without any doubt that I was called to ministry.

The internship had helped me see that I wanted to serve in a local church (I had a friend who was serving as a community college chaplain), but I was not comfortable stating that I had been "called." This language seemed presumptuous to me—to declare without any reservations that I knew God wanted me to do this. I was pursuing ordained ministry partly because of my own need to grow; I was not confident it was God's initiative. Also, I felt that I was not a better person than other lay people I knew, so how could I ask to be—as UMC ordination stated—"set apart" from them? I did not like the way that sounded.

I needed time. One day, a colleague named Betsy Alden helped me. She said, "God has given you certain gifts. Your gifts are not necessarily better than others—all our gifts are needed—but the church benefits from people with gifts like yours, using these gifts in full-time service."

It was true. I had a certain gift for speaking and writing, and I had a hunger for spiritual growth that was fueling my entire journey through seminary and into ministry. These gifts could be of use to a local church. Beyond that, I had a gift for cultivating relationships and connecting with strangers because of a deep love I have for people in general. If ministry is all about relationships, maybe my path really was leading me to the local church.

Betsy continued, "You are also getting confirmation of your call to ministry—and your gifts—through the ordination process as you go before pastors and lay people who are challenging you with good questions before affirming your call."

Her explanation made sense to me. I had entered this entire process to learn and explore—not with the certainty of some of my male friends who had been preaching in small churches on the weekends for some time and had been mentored by older men to "go into the ministry." I had come in open but with no mentors. I needed to find my own way, and along the way, God and I seemed to be coming together. Or maybe I stood still long enough for God to finally catch up with me.

Either way, I had peace when I went before the North Texas Conference of The United Methodist Church Board of Ordained Ministry and replied to their opening question about my call, "Yes, I am called to serve God—not myself—to do what He wants me to do and be. If that is full-time work in the church, I am ready to go, ready to move into uncharted waters, ready to trust that all will work out for good." With Don's encouragement, I took the leap, and even though there were many challenges along the way, I have never again doubted that it was God who called me, prompted me, and said to me, "You have to do this." I was no longer in charge; God had moved into that role.

Divine Intervention
When I finished my internship at Highland Park United Methodist Church, I hoped that I could stay on there as the four male interns had done before me. I thought it would be the perfect place to begin ministry. And maybe it would have been, except when I went in to meet with the senior pastor at the time, Dr. Leighton Farrell, who was kind, but firm, he said, "There are no positions available on the staff. My suggestion is for you to reach out to some other churches."

I was so disappointed and felt rejected; why couldn't he create a new position? Yet it had also been his decision to bring me on as an intern, which had been a wonderful gift. So, I decided to take his advice and move on. Soon I interviewed for an associate pastor position at Christ United Methodist Church in Plano where my husband, Don, and I were attending at the time. Again, I was confident it was the right place for me—especially since the staff knew me. But after wrestling with the decision, the committee chose the other candidate, a male that I knew well from seminary. This time I was devastated, and I cried all night, heartbroken and grief-stricken about the rejection. Couldn't they see I was perfect for that position?

I woke up the next morning and did a wise thing; I stopped crying long enough to listen. God spoke to me clearly, and I finally heard, as *She* told me that there was another United Methodist Church in town that had just started, and it might be looking for help.

People often sing in worship the words "God will make a way," and that way came in the fall of 1980 through a part-time position at Custer Road United Methodist Church in Plano. All that worrying I had done about having to uproot our family so I could go where I was sent was a waste of energy. By nothing short of divine intervention, Custer Road UMC was located just four miles from our house. When I called to talk to the pastor, Rev. Mark Craig, I volunteered to work at the church for free. That was the right thing to say to a church that was just beginning to get traction, and Mark preached about that conversation for years to come in his sermons, endearing me to the congregation. Soon I hit the ground running, not working for free after all, but on the move and in the middle of the action.

Could it be that this God I served really did know best?

Entering the Clergy Ranks
Despite a lack of women in ministry at the time, The United

Methodist Church formally welcomed me into its ranks. In June 1980, I was ordained a deacon, which was the first step, and the final step came in 1983 when I was ordained an elder. I was a colleague to my male counterparts, but unlike them, I was a daughter, a wife, a mom, and a sister. My journey had been shaped by being a woman, and I brought all that life experience into this new arena.

I still had lots of doubts and questions, and I'd come to this game later in life than most—at age 37. Yet, as the seventh woman to be ordained in the North Texas Conference of The United Methodist Church, I was welcomed and blessed—questions and all.

It was a high and holy moment on a very warm spring night in May 1983, at First United Methodist Church in Wichita Falls, Texas, when I was ordained an elder. We processed down the long center aisle, and I remember noticing the stained-glass windows and beautiful chandeliers. There was a big crowd, and most of my family were there, including Don, Wendi, and Trey.

Dr. Will Willimon was the preacher for the evening. He looked very official in his black clerical robe with three stripes on the side and colorful vestments. In addition to being a preacher, he was also an author, and I had read several of his books. His irony and sense of humor always spoke to me. I was thrilled he had been chosen to preach that year, for he was one of the colleagues I admired the most. He preached on the parable of the Good Samaritan in Luke 10. Dr Willimon summarized, "You are called to love your neighbor, not so much to be successful. Your neighbor is anyone of any race, creed, or social background who is in need. Loving them means you act to meet the need."

Hymns were played, the choir sung, scripture was read, and when it came time to kneel and have hands laid on me by the bishop, I was open to receiving the blessing. I felt the Presence—the Holy Spirit—and in that moment, what I desired for my life lined up with what I believed God was calling me to do. Was I ready? I hoped so. The equally important question was whether the church was ready for me.

Keeping It Simple

In an effort to keep up with the strong growth in the Dallas suburbs during the early 1980s, The North Texas Conference of The United Methodist Church was eager to start new churches. Custer Road United Methodist Church was their top choice for a potential "poster child" for church starts, so they had invested in five acres—instead of the usual two or three—on Custer Road, a major street running north and south through the community of west Plano, an up-and-coming part of suburbia. It was the place to be for white, middle-class professionals looking for a strong public school system for their children in a somewhat homogenous environment.

On February 10, 1980, the church held its first worship service at Thomas Elementary, a school in the Plano Independent School District. I started my first week as an associate pastor at Custer Road UMC when it was still meeting at the elementary school. Rev. Mark Craig, the pastor I was working with, was a strong, passionate, and energetic leader who had grown up in Fort Worth, Texas, and then graduated from Duke Divinity School before returning to North Texas. He was slightly bald at the time, with brown eyes and a sense of urgency about everything he did. He also had a good professional reputation, and I was soon to see why.

Mark had the right combination of skills and intellect for starting a new church. He was a good communicator—really good at preaching to unchurched males, which was a large part of our target audience in the predominately white suburbs like Plano. He had a 1-2-3 approach which was easy to remember, and best of all, he used humor in all the right places. His stories reminded me how good laughter was, especially at church where we could easily become too serious.

I remember Mark preaching about his car—the one he drove that first year while he was visiting people. "I love my 1970 Ford Fairlane," he said. Then he added, "I have problems with my doors, though. Both front doors don't open much of the time. So, when this happens, I must get in through the back seat, hoping like crazy that no one sees me while I crawl into the front seat. When I am visiting potential members, I have learned to park way down the street out of sight." The congregation burst into laughter. This story got him a lot of traction—also attention and sympathy—and everyone was relieved when he bought a new car, one with doors that worked!

I, on the other hand, showed up to Custer Road with a car that was in good shape, but with my own challenge—I was a woman preacher at a time when this was very rare. I was eager to prove myself as a graduate of a rather progressive seminary about 20 miles south of the church and very grateful to have employment so close to home. I was ready to do my part in this new endeavor, which I assumed would be first about connecting with people and then building relationships. I was really hoping that this would be one of my strengths, because I could see all these people pouring into Plano, most of them without a church home. A few of them were in my neighborhood.

Not everyone looked favorably on a female pastor in those days, but I felt instantly accepted because Mark was so confident that I was the one for the job. I wasn't much of a threat to the congregation, either, because I was truly there to serve the church and connect with people. It helped that I had arrived while the church was still on the ground floor and new families with children were joining our ranks. Everyone was excited to see what was in store for Custer Road, and they seemed open to new possibilities—like women preachers!

Mark was the entrepreneur, always on the go, and obsessed with being efficient and effective. My role was to help with worship and build the infrastructure of the congregation. I was tasked with connecting people and starting Sunday school classes. We complemented each other well, and I took great joy over the years when people would tell me that they joined the church because of Mark and stayed because of me.

My office for the first two years was in a small trailer on the five acres purchased by The United Methodist North Texas Conference. Inside that one room, Mark and I each had a phone and a desk; that was it. In those early days, there was a humility and a simplicity in the church that I liked—for this seemed to fit who I was at that point.

Joan Newman, the administrative assistant, had worked in the conference office and understood the church at every level. She was mature, in her 50s, had a round face with a sparkle in her eyes and knew how to speak very softly but very clearly. Even more important, she knew how to keep Mark—and me—out of trouble with the United Methodist hierarchy, which took a great deal of savvy on her part since we did not usually follow the rules or have all the meetings the conference suggested.

I never questioned Joan in administrative matters. She could open the file drawer near her desk and immediately pull out any number or statistic that I needed—far better than any computer. In later years, she became not only the chief administrator but also the key communicator to lay people and staff. She provided a welcoming place where anyone could ask questions about what was going on in the church—while Mark and I were running around, always on the go, carrying out one task or another.

He and I were both very focused and intense—too much at times—wanting to move forward and reach new people. One of the reasons my work was so fulfilling was that I was starting new things—new classes, new groups, new ministries, and new initiatives. It gave me energy; I would start a ministry or class, turn it over to the lay leaders when they were ready, and then move on to begin another ministry. It proved to be a great way to assimilate new people and to build our leadership base.

The teamwork made the dream work at Custer Road United Methodist Church. We exploded on the scene. Exactly 240 people came to that very first service at the elementary school on a snowy Texas day. It was nothing short of a miracle because Texans do *not* like to drive when it's icy outside. Within months, membership was growing so much we had to move to Carpenter Middle School, and during the summer we held Vacation Bible School in a local park. By that time, my part-time position had become a full-time position—with a raise!

We had to get serious about planning a dedicated church facility from the very beginning, and we were proud to see phase one completed in 1983—a multipurpose building that later became the fellowship hall. We had no clue that this was just the first phase of six phases for a church startup that would grow to meet the needs of thousands of individuals and families for decades to come.

We were off to a strong start thanks to Mark's tenacity and willingness to meet with families and invite them to church. By the time we had entered phase one and moved from the elementary school to the new building, we were already using every square inch of space we could find for worship and for Sunday School classes—including the kitchen, our offices, hall space, even off-campus. Custer Road became the place to be on Sunday mornings.

2,000 members called Custer Road home by 1986, the same year we opened a new Education Building and started a church library. 500 children came to our pre-school program each week—the largest program of its kind in Plano, Texas. In what can only be described as God's idea, our facilities were built on the spout of Spring Creek, a natural spring that gave us a bit of trouble in the beginning, but in a special way reflected exactly the role our budding church served in our community—a wellspring of life and joy that never stopped flowing.

Approximately ten years after we began working together, Mark invited me into Joan's office one morning and said to the two of us, "Seventeen acres have become available for sale near our property. It is right up the street. Do you think the church should buy it?" Without any hesitation, both of us said "Yes!" He got up from the desk and went downtown and bought the land. That was on a Friday, and on Sunday morning, he announced the purchase to the congregation. I remember wondering—but for only a moment, "Should we have checked that out with anyone in the congregation?"

No one ever questioned it or the other decisions we made. The church now had 22 acres instead of five. Obviously, we worked in a high-trust environment with a few people making decisions. We did not get bogged down in committee meetings or administrative items; we were moving forward and reaching new people.

A major milestone came in 1990 with the completion of the Custer Road sanctuary. Just ten years after meeting in an elementary school, we had completed our mission of getting the church fully off the ground and into its beautiful new home.

Birthing Place

In so many ways Custer Road UMC was my birthing place. The congregation understood that I was new to all this church stuff, and they took it easy on me, seldom criticizing when I made mistakes. And I certainly made them. One of those times happened in the first year, 1980, when the church was still meeting at Thomas Elementary. In the midst of preaching on Communion Sunday about Paul's words to the church in Corinth, I had just said something like, "He will strengthen you..." before dropping my notes onto the floor and losing my place. (I had stayed up late the night before, changing my sermon at the last minute—not a good idea.)

I stumbled through the rest of the sermon—so embarrassed and humiliated. I had let the congregation down; I felt terrible. In fact, I was in pain. When the sermon was finally over and they came up for Communion, several of them stopped and did a wonderful thing. They looked me in the eye and hugged me. I felt forgiven. Did I ever need that. I was still loved! Some of the awful pain went away, and I could live to preach again.

I was learning that grace is life-giving. The laity actually loved me as I was. They loved me when I talked too much or too loudly, when I worried about the wrong things, when I was impatient—even demanding—about tasks, when I wanted to get credit for something, when I tried to get things done too quickly, and when I was too direct—even blunt—in asking for money.

I remember calling one of the women lay leaders one day and without explaining very much, I asked her for a large donation to some project. I don't remember if she gave a gift or not, but I do remember that she was very caring and asked me, "Donna, are you OK?" I realized that I had not hidden the panic and anxiety in my voice very well, and more important than the gift was the fact that she cared about me.

Because I was loved by the congregation, those first years in ministry were a time where I could risk and fail, where I could be forgiven, where I could slip and fall—as I literally did once in the entrance for a wedding—and they would pick me up. They were good sports about being stuck in portable buildings for years, while the church built one building after another. They trusted the staff, and we trusted them—a priceless gift.

They also embraced and loved my family, gave them a place to be themselves, and welcomed them into the church community. My daughter, Wendi, was in fifth grade and my son, Trey, was in first grade when I started at Custer Road. Like many preacher's kids, Wendi didn't particularly want to stand out and said once, "I wish people in Sunday School wouldn't expect me to know a lot about the Bible."

Trey responded a little differently, remarking years later, "My youth group was the only place in my life where I could truly be myself—no pretense, no fakeness, no putting on a mask."

My husband, Don, was loved and affirmed, and some of our most special—even holy—family moments were shared at the church: third-grade Bible presentations, sixth-grade confirmation, high school graduations, Wendi's wedding, Wendi's personal encouragement by a wonderful Sunday School teacher named Becky Moore, Trey playing Joseph in a Christmas pageant, Wendi's friends at church who were in her wedding, Trey being a part of youth choir concerts, and both of them going on ski trips. Today they laugh about the fact they would often go to my office and "worship" there rather than be seen by others in the sanctuary. There were definite advantages—and disadvantages—to having a mom for a preacher, and they were learning to lean into the advantages.

Knowing I Need Others
John Wesley, founder of the Methodist movement (which grew into numerous churches throughout the world, including the United Methodist Church of today), strongly rejected the thinking that people can be mature people of faith without understanding how much we need each other. His famous class meetings reinforced the truth of these words: "Remember you cannot serve Him (God) alone. You

must therefore find companions or make them. The Bible knows nothing of solitary religion."

I began to learn this life-transforming lesson at Custer Road UMC. Family members, friends, colleagues and others had gifts and wisdom that I did not have, and that was a good thing. We had so much to learn from each other. When I invested in key relationships, I became more human, more alive, and hopefully more empathetic.

I found that some of my closest friends through the years—the ones I could really count on—were parents of children who were in the same grade as my two children or who were on the same sports team. We had a strong bond because of our children, and that bond remained after the children graduated. I can call several of them if I need help with almost anything today, for the important part is that we learned to trust one another and count on each other.

I realized that the church could be that kind of community—a place with small groups and classes where individuals learn to be vulnerable and honest with one another as they are learning to be real in their relationship with God. As trust deepens, it becomes easier to see God at work and hear God nudge us to be or do more. We can have a positive impact on each other because we are encouraging and inspiring one another. Others have inspired me through the years, and I want to pass that kind of encouragement along to those who are ready.

It thrills me that sometimes I can affirm others as they discover their call. Five or six women at Custer Road UMC felt called to pursue full-time ministry in The United Methodist Church during the years I was there. One of those was Jan Davis. Jan came into my office one day in the early '90s. She began, "I am struggling. I do not know whether to have a third child or pursue a call to ministry."

"You know, the two are not mutually exclusive," I replied.

"Hmmm." Jan responded.

She was about the same age I was when I had struggled with my call to ministry. Before she left, we agreed that she could do both. She went on to thrive in seminary and beyond, becoming the senior pastor of what was at that time the largest United Methodist Church in our jurisdiction. Even more important, she had a third daughter who grew up to be an engineer like her dad. I am grateful for Jan's friendship and proud of her incredible ministry that is impacting so many people.

We all need each other.

And dare I say it—and only slightly tongue in cheek—it is now time for women clergy to use their unique gifts to wade into the water and tackle the issues of our time in an appropriate way—to speak up and speak out through preaching and leading. And so, I did.

Chapter Five
Preach It

Religion is at its best when it makes us ask hard questions of ourselves. It is at its worst when it deludes us into thinking we have all the answers for everyone else.

—Archibald MacLeish

Preach It, Sister

I had taken courses about the art of preaching at seminary, but it was at Custer Road that I actually learned to preach. The church became a kind of training ground for me, a place to take risks. I had always liked to teach, but preaching was different—more challenging. It involved listening to God, not just gathering information.

The approach I developed was to begin with a question that emerged from the text and then lift up three to four responses from the scripture. I wanted to engage the congregation the same way Rev. Bourdon Smith had engaged me in those early days in Richardson. I wanted worshipers to love scripture as much as I did, to see how much it speaks to us today. I wanted to make the message simple, so there was a clear takeaway. I wanted the gospel to change lives like it was changing mine.

I preached almost 200 sermons at Custer Road UMC, but it was never easy. Since Mark and I were the only ordained ministers for the first ten years, I was often the one who preached when he was gone. I enjoyed the process and what I learned in preparing, but I enjoyed it even more when the sermon was over. I'd fret over it the week before, allowing it to consume all my time. Adding to the pressure was the fact that Mark did not use notes. I wanted to do the same thing, so I would spend my Saturdays memorizing my sermon, praying that I would remember it on Sunday mornings.

I was pretty good at telling other people's stories. I found my favorite storytellers were those who spoke from the heart, like Will Willimon, Frederick Buechner, Walter Wangerin, Philip Yancey, and later Liz Curtis Higgs. (I wished I could find more women.) If I cried when I read their stories, I knew they were good ones because the Holy Spirit was speaking. It took me years to realize that I had good stories of my own to tell; in fact, they were often the best ones. But in those early days, I held back. That kind of honesty came in later years as I learned to trust that those stories that I told which were the most personal were usually the ones that were also the most universal. I was learning to be more vulnerable—and in the process, becoming more human.

I remember one of the first stories about myself that I shared with the congregation. I related in great detail my entrance into a wedding that I was conducting at Custer Road. (My son, Trey, was in the wedding party but had not come in with the procession yet.) I had bought new high heels for this special occasion. It was during that silent and holy time of a wedding when the pastor comes in to wait for the processional to begin and everyone—I mean everyone—had their eyes on me.

The spiky heels caught on the steps before I reached the altar. I tripped and fell hard. It made a very loud sound, and the whole congregation gasped in horror. I got up immediately, was not hurt, but was *so* embarrassed and humiliated. I wanted to disappear. As I told this story, the congregation laughed, enjoying this lighter moment in the sermon, and I was able to laugh, too—I think for the first time.

The Woman Question

Weddings at the church were a big part of our family's social life. I presided over many of them, and sometimes the "woman question" popped up. I had been at the church less than a year when Mark was going out of town and asked me to conduct a wedding ceremony in the home of a member who was very traditional in her views, particularly regarding the role of women in the church.

Later she told me that she pitched a fit when she discovered that a woman would be doing the wedding instead of Mark, saying to her friends, "We might as well not even have it!" Maybe it is good that I had no idea how she felt. I showed up and presided over the wedding, thinking what a great experience the whole wedding was. In the next few years, she and I became close friends, as did our children. We both laugh each time I go to her home, remembering the first time we met and the unknown—on my part—tension that was in the air. Sometimes innocence is bliss.

Another time I was the host pastor doing a wedding with a pastor from a rather conservative denomination. During the service, I gave the couple the wedding vows, and the other pastor proceeded to ignore what I had done and gave the vows all over again. He acted as if what I had done did not count!

Overall, however, I have great memories of the many couples I married during that season of my ministry, including the weddings of many of the friends of my children. There was something very special about that time in my ministry—I could be both pastor and friend, and it made all of us feel like one big family. Our children went to school together; the parents all went to sporting events together, and everybody went to church together.

Funerals brought a different kind of challenge—and opportunity. I found that if I was available to a family in a time of need, it really did not matter if I were a woman or a man. People just wanted someone they could trust, someone who cared about them and who could help them get through the loss.

One of my first funerals was a service for a high school student who committed suicide, the daughter of one of our members. The entire community of Plano was reeling because several young people in a rather short period of time had done the same thing. People were hurting and scared. I realized that my role was to care for them, to give hope and to preach the gospel—to drive home that God's love is unconditional and all-embracing, and that God understands and accepts when human beings might not.

It was through presiding over funerals that I learned to be a pastor—someone who cared, who was available, who could express love at the right time, someone who could be fully present. I would go see the family, and there would be lots of laughing and crying and telling stories together. Then during the service, I would tell a few of those stories, remembering what my Aunt Berta always said, "Donna, don't make the person into something they were not." In other words, keep it real.

Then would come the good news that the best is yet to come—no separation from God and the saints who have gone before us, the promise of life after death. I could feel the sigh of relief coming from the congregation. In time I learned that the service was not so much about my preaching as it was about a dialogue going on between the people in the congregation and me. They participated *with* me in the grieving, in the celebration of the person's life, in the anticipation of what was ahead.

On the Move

Mark and I were proud—a little too proud—of our lean-and-mean approach to growing the church, especially when it came to staffing. From the first time the church met on February 10, 1980, I was the only other full-time staff person until 1985. We made a priority of building, staying with the basics, and starting new classes. This was all good because we were blessed with good timing. It was the beginning of Plano's glory days. However, we probably took it too far.

The church did not hire a full-time director of music until 1985—Tim Morrison—and a full-time director of youth ministry, John Baldwin, in 1989. Every other staff person for approximately the first ten years was part-time. Morrison used his unending energy to build the adult choir and grow the music ministry, but his greatest strength was involving hundreds of youth in summer musicals like *Godspell* and helping them uncover their ability to sing, dance, and act. My son Trey was one of those—although Trey drove Tim and me crazy by always waiting to the last minute to learn his lines.

Morrison and Baldwin worked well together, and over time developed the strongest youth ministry in North Texas at that time with a total of 675 youth coming on Sunday mornings and Sunday and Wednesday evenings. Mark and I were very focused also, and I look back on those days with great fondness. We were in the zone.

Always wanting to be efficient and effective, the church decided to build an education building in 1985 instead of a sanctuary, making room for Sunday School classes and more small groups. Finally in 1990, it was time to build the sanctuary, ten years after I had arrived on the scene. Our plan? A classy, beautiful, traditional design with a center aisle. The problem? The contracted architectural firm delivered a design that was modern, eight-sided in shape, without a steeple or a front door. It looked more like an airport than a traditional church.

Our building committee suffered through many long meetings before voting to release the original architects; it was only in later years that I realized how pivotal this move was in solidifying the traditional identity of the church. In fact, Custer Road set the pace; over the next several years, the three other United Methodist churches in town all built beautiful traditional sanctuaries, and Plano became a great and exciting place for United Methodists.

May 11, 1990, was the Saturday before our first Sunday in the new sanctuary. I stood in the balcony taking everything in. I was overwhelmed with joy and gratitude. It seemed that all the work of the first ten years was paying off. The steeple had been erected, and the room was stunning—beautiful, with a center aisle and eight stained-glass front doors opening out to Custer Road. No one had to ask, "Where is the front door?"

Custer Road UMC was growing—and hopefully maturing—as a congregation, with more than 800 people now attending Sunday School and a music program that had grown to include five choirs. The church had installed an organ from Lovers Lane UMC in Dallas—perhaps a hint from God about where my path would eventually lead. Kay Sendrey was a great organist—a people person who could play all kinds of music—traditional, contemporary, gospel, and whatever Tim came up with. She invited hundreds of people of all ages to participate in the worship service by either singing or playing a musical instrument. Many of the adults would start out by saying, "I am not a trained musician," but soon she would have them up in front of the church doing their part. It worked, and I loved the casual music atmosphere where so many people participated and found their way of serving.

Mark spearheaded a new mission initiative—a Friday night respite program for parents of special needs children, and Stephanie Mills came on board as the right lay person to expand the outreach ministry of the church. (I am happy to say she is still there.) The church was beginning to get national recognition. In 1988, *The Dallas Morning News* named Custer Road UMC the "Silver Lining in the Methodist Church," tempting the staff to believe that we were good at this church growth thing with our great plans, projects, and priorities. Did we need to be humbled?

One night after the DMN article came out—during the closing out of our annual fundraising campaign—the stewardship team was gathered in the sanctuary. We were using the traditional Methodist circuit rider approach where a saddlebag with a commitment card is moved from one house to another until every family is contacted. All members of the team were waiting for one last set of cards to come in. The commitments were $25,000 short of our goal, and it was time to go home. As the chair of the campaign walked over to turn off the lights for the night, the last saddlebag came in. The team stayed to open the bag, AND—wonder of wonders—the total committed was exactly $25,000. Not a penny more, not a penny less.

I couldn't believe it—right down to the exact penny. I thought, "God, is this how You remind us that You are around? Is this how You get our attention? Because if it is, it is working." I had recently read in an article, "God never comes late, but He doesn't come early. He always comes right on time." I will never forget that night. It made a big impression on me. For the first time in a long time, I saw how much time I spent at the church planning and managing and executing and doing and how little time I spent listening to God. Did I really want to be known primarily as someone who knew how to grow a church and raise money, or did I want to be known as someone who was learning to trust God more?

Even more important, could I let go of my strong need to be successful and admired by others as a church growth expert so that I might find a deeper purpose and calling? I caught a glimpse of how privileged I had become with my comfortable, suburban lifestyle and how much time and money I was spending on things I wanted and convinced myself that I needed. Had I forgotten what Willimon said in my ordination service? "It is not about success; it is about serving God and meeting the needs of my neighbors."

"Hmmm..." became the soundtrack for my growing pains.

Truth Found in Paradox and Continuum
It was at Custer Road that I first learned the importance of having what I call "bridge people" in the life of a church and in our own lives as well. Through the years I saw this gift in the lives of several women and men I respected—people like Eugene Peterson, Beth Moore, Rachel Evans, Richard Rohr,

African Bishop Muyambo, and many others. These leaders unite or bring together two worlds that others often separate.

Bridge people bring new energy into traditional ways of thinking and tend to be comfortable with struggling instead of having to be certain. Most of all, they listen to the inner voice—the Holy Spirit—and in doing this, become change agents for those who need change the most, those on the margins.

Our churches can then be exciting places to be when we as church pastors move beyond the role of being chaplains for the middle class—who tend to be comfortable with the status quo—to becoming friends and guides for those who are ready to make a change in their lives.

As a pastor I am still learning how important it is to understand both sides of an issue and to become a bridge person myself when needed. I want to be able to practice active listening, where I repeat what I understand another person to be saying, showing them that they have been heard and validated.

And in the last few years, I am working harder at seeing ideas not so much as opposites that are in tension with one another but as polarities that move along a continuum, moving slowly from one end to another, changing slightly as they move along, sometimes closer to one end, sometimes closer to the other. This kind of movement brings breathing room into a discussion that might be divisive.

I am glad that John Wesley thought like this because he encouraged people to learn from others, not to just argue with them. He was comfortable examining his own views. For example, he once stated that he wanted to "retract several expressions" in the hymns he wrote because he had shifted in what he believed about Christian perfection. (Rev. John Wesley, *A Plain Account of Christian Perfection* [G.A. Lane and P.P. Sandford, 1844], 124)

He was comfortable changing and evolving. It seems that the greatest enemy of our time is extremism and rigidity of thought—drawing a line in the sand and saying it is absolute truth. The ego hates, more than anything else, to change. Rather than die to the illusion it believes in, the ego wants to make predictability and control more important than listening. The Holy Spirit, however, is available and wants to be heard.

I have also learned that being faithful does not mean being certain all the time. "I don't know" is a perfectly acceptable response. At Custer Road, I began to seek the kind of deep wisdom and humility that comes from knowing what I don't know.

In the end, I came to believe that ultimate Truth—with a capital T—can only be found in the person of Jesus. Truth, then, is not a proposition or a doctrine or a certain way of interpreting scripture. Truth is the way of life that Jesus showed us. No wonder that Jesus often communicated through stories, parables, metaphors, and even riddles. It is no surprise that Jesus seemed to be comfortable with mystery and that which is always unfolding. He didn't seem to be concerned about using precise or exact words—he was more concerned with the spirit behind the words. He told and showed his disciples this again and again.

Isn't it freeing that Jesus left room for more than one way of interpreting His words and stories? Again, John Wesley said to think and let think. And when it comes to the hot button issues of our day, like homosexuality, Jesus never spoke about that topic, so it must not have been a central issue for him. Could we honor Him by giving each other a little grace on this and go easy on one another?

I was realizing that this is what soul work is all about—listening, respecting, learning to love more.

New Space for New People

In 1992, two years after the sanctuary opened at Custer Road UMC, the church leaders had a similar opportunity to go deeper, pause and reflect—to decide what kind of church they were going to be. Like an individual who is growing and changing, I wondered if the church was mature enough to think of others' needs more than its own, to do some soul work.

The vision that God had given Mark for Custer Road UMC had worked from the start—worship and Sunday

I Am Enough

School would go hand in hand to reach the unchurched. It was the church's mission—short and to the point, Mark's style. He and I had been able to do our thing and help carry out this mission without much discomfort—certainly not sacrifice—on our part or on the part of the congregation. I was thrilled to see new people coming through the doors of the new sanctuary. It hit me (now I know it was God speaking) that it was time for us to create space for new people through additional Sunday Schools and small groups. Who could help?

Of course, my Baptist colleagues could and would. They were good at church growth and were eager to share their methods. I reached out to them, and they helped me to see that Custer Road UMC could add a second Sunday School hour at a time that was convenient for new people. I thought this sounded like a good plan. Could the church stretch, change its habits, and be other-oriented by moving to a different hour? I started reading books and articles on leading people through change, for I sensed the church was about to enter some possible conflict and potentially dangerous territory.

I was right about that.

At this point our church had 20 adult Sunday School classes, and it was maxed out in our building; if a new Sunday School hour was added, the church could add new classes without having to build more space. A major decision was the time of the new Sunday School hour. Initially believing that it should be at 11, after checking with other churches, it became clear that an earlier time, 8:30, would work better. It sounded simple, but it was not.

I soon had to come to grips with the fact that the church culture of my Baptist colleagues was different from United Methodists. While Baptist members are more likely to follow the lead of their pastors in a time of expansion when the pastor says, "This is the way that the church is going to do this," United Methodists tend to be more independent and free-thinking, asking lots of questions—good questions.

Early in the process I presented the idea to Mark who said something like, "Sure, the church needs to grow. Go with it." I appreciated the fact that he was leaving the details up to me. Nine months later, after many leaders were fully committed to the change, a long-established Sunday School class went to him and complained about the inconvenience of what they called a "disruption." They had settled into their routine and did not want to change the meeting time. Mark called me in and asked if I could call the whole thing off. I had to say to him that it was too late. *Ugh!*

The support I needed came from Joan, the savvy business administrator who was one of the first ones to see why the church needed to grow in this way. When the rest of the staff started resisting, she calmly replied, "If you want a full-time job here five years from now, you need to get with this vision." That threat worked; the staff got on board.

This was a significant initiative, one that impacted the church's growth for the next two decades and beyond. Best of all, new space was created for new people, and they came pouring in.

I was riding high, believing that I had displayed great leadership and impressed my colleagues. Sunday School attendance increased from around 1,300 to 1,700 by the end of 1993, moving to 2,000 by the end of 1995. Worship attendance reached almost 5,000. Mark wrote an article about me for our church newsletter calling me his "right hand man" in the building of the church, and we were forging ahead. With so many things going well, what could go wrong?

Chapter Six
End of the Beginning

...the characteristics in human nature which we love best grow in a soil with a strong mixture of trouble.

—*Harry Emerson Fosdick*

Shocked and Unsettled

It was early February 1995, and the church was in its 15th year. I had been out of town. When I drove into the parking lot of the church, one of my colleagues, who was just about to get in his car, said to me, "Have you talked to Mark? He has something important to tell you."

This colleague sounded very serious, and I soon learned why. The United Methodist Church has an appointive system, and Mark had been appointed by our conference cabinet—a bishop and six district superintendents—to become senior pastor of Highland Park UMC in Dallas, the largest church in the conference and one of the top two United Methodist churches in the country. It was the church where I had done my internship. I knew the conference had made the appointment, but I also knew that Mark had to say yes to it.

I was shocked and unsettled. I had not seen this coming, but as I reflected, I remembered he had hinted at a change about two weeks before this, and I had not paid much attention to it. Now all I could think was how could he leave something that was going so well—especially when he and I were still at the top of our game? I had envisioned an exciting future with the church—and with Mark—continuing to expand all the good missions and ministries the staff had started with him at the helm. Now everything was up in the air. And I had no control over any of it.

In one sense, I knew everything would be "fine" with or without Mark—as the lay leaders went around saying—reassuring everyone that Custer Road UMC was a formidable church with a solid leadership base and that our identity was set. I, too, went around trying to act as if his unexpected departure was no big deal, but inside I was in deep grief and scared of what lay ahead. In fact, it seems that I, too, did not like change.

End of the Beginning

I was not particularly pastoral to the congregation during this season, especially those who were angry or felt abandoned by Mark. I knew I needed to be positive because most people—at least on the surface—were ready to wish Mark well. I remember in my better moments saying something like, "His leaving is not the end, but it is the end of the beginning." No matter that none of us had any idea what the ending—or the new beginning—would look like.

And no one knew how to grieve the loss of this father figure who had placed his durable stamp on the face of our church family. So, we ignored or denied any pain involved in his leaving. There were no good consultants or counselors around to remind us how important it is to say good-bye. I did not know enough about transitions to ask for help, and the conference did not offer any. The church stumbled forward on its own.

I kept thinking about how much of the identity of the church was grounded in who Mark was, what he valued, what his priorities were. He was the founding pastor. Would the church lose its identity after he was gone? In business terms, Mark was a big success. I saw him as our unorthodox, storytelling, high-energy, quick-decision-making preacher and colleague. Almost everyone—including me—loved his craziness, willingness to take risks, and gift of starting a church that had grown so rapidly. Could he be replaced? Could the church go on without him? "Yes!" was everyone's answer, but I was not sure. I did not have enough faith to hear that there was a bigger plan at work. This change was painful, and I did not like pain.

Looking back, I realize I placed much too high expectations on Mark throughout the transition. While I knew he cared a great deal about the church, I also wanted him to care deeply about taking care of the congregation and staff—those he was leaving behind. I wanted him to make a big deal of saying good-bye and bless the congregation before he left. I wanted him to celebrate with all of us what the church had accomplished working together through the years. I wanted to hear him say how much he was going to miss everyone, including me. I wanted him to acknowledge that I had been his partner through it all.

He did none of that, said no formal goodbyes. Instead, he focused on his next exciting challenge—about the most exciting challenge a United Methodist Church pastor could have in our denomination. He was embarrassed and uncomfortable when people got too close or emotional—he is an introvert—so he simply cut ties and "got the hell out of Dodge," announcing an immediate three-month sabbatical to prepare for his new appointment.

That might have been good for Mark, but it was not good for our congregation. There were very few things about the transition in the spring of 1995 that went smoothly. Neither the staff nor the laity were prepared for such an abrupt ending, and everyone struggled through it in his or her own way without having any kind of closure. When Mark left so rapidly, I was put in charge. Unfortunately, things heated up a little when two other pastors on the staff thought they should be in charge instead of me. Do I need to say they were men?

The Custer Road UMC staff parish relations committee sent out a letter clarifying my role, and things calmed down. However, there were potential land mines everywhere—so many ways to make a mistake, to say the wrong thing, to say things in the wrong way. The staff was on edge, wondering who and what was ahead. I remember times that a few of us made guesses about possibilities for our next pastor, trying to be light-hearted about the change. It was a good way of dealing with the anxiety, because we needed to laugh. One thing was for sure; we had no say in what was ahead. The UMC North Texas Conference cabinet members were the decision makers. Time to get with the program—and pray.

New Man in Town

The cabinet was embarking on one of its biggest searches yet. It was a search for a leader, just the right one, to move Custer Road UMC into the next two decades of being "church." With an extremely strong foundation in both worship and Sunday School and small groups, the church was expecting the best.

During the spring of 1995, I heard about one—and then another—pastor being considered for Custer Road UMC. In the end, I was relieved when the cabinet chose Rev. Paul Goodrich, who arrived in June 1995. When he arrived, Custer Road was no longer the new church in town. The Southern Baptists, Presbyterians, Episcopalians, Catholics, and others had all followed us into the fertile territory of northwest Plano. Since many of the other churches grew rapidly, Plano was blessed with many different denominations and faith traditions. Ours was not the only steeple in town.

I liked what I knew about Paul and was intrigued by the appointment. I knew he was an experienced churchman with a father who had made it big in the church world as a pastor of First UMC in Dallas before becoming a bishop. Paul was one of several sons in our conference whose fathers were well-known and respected preachers. It did help to have connections.

However, Paul had paid his dues. He was known as a good guy and company man who served in small churches before ending up in a large church in Wichita Falls. I was soon to discover that he was non-anxious for the most part, laid back in many ways, and comfortable in his own skin. In fact, one of his greatest strengths was that he made no effort to be like Mark—to preach like him, to make quick decisions like him, to keep the lay administrative structure small as he had done. Paul was different, and he was comfortable being different.

I realized that the days of the three of us—Mark, Joan, and me—making all the decisions and then sharing it with the congregation were gone. Paul was more consensus driven. I knew that this change was good in some ways; it was healthy to take a deep breath, but I felt everything was slowing down. In fact, I felt myself slowing down too, and I was not sure how I felt about it. Slowing down was different, even uncomfortable. Could I adapt?

I did like the relaxed aspect of Paul. I had never seen myself as anxious—of course, I never looked at anything about myself that could be negative—but observing his laid-back approach helped me realize how task-driven I had been. Paul had no need to impress, and he showed class by moving into Mark's very small office away from the center of the action. "Why did Mark want such a small office?" he asked.

"He is an introvert," I responded. "Mark was great in the pulpit with 2,000 people each Sunday but not very interested in one-on-one conversations with members. He had an unusual schedule—was a great father—and was not actually at the church that much. He left most of the daily operations of running the church to Joan and me. And the two of us were pretty good at it."

In a short time, Paul became a wonderful colleague and friend. I think he and I knew how much we needed each other. I needed him to help the congregation stay confident about the big change in leadership it was going through, and he needed me to be the glue that helped keep things together until Custer Road could regain some stability. In family systems language, the mobile was shaking—a lot. I moved into my connecting and encouragement mode.

Stumbling

In 1996, one year after Paul came and 16 years after I came to Custer Road UMC, my whole world changed; my father died after a brief illness. I was about to enter my fifth decade of life. I had been with several people in the congregation as they were dying, and I thought I knew how to "handle" death.

I was wrong. I had been protected and sheltered much of my life, and I had little experience with bad things happening to good people in my own family. I also did not know myself well enough to understand my tendency to avoid or deny negative news, especially news that I did not want to hear—even when reality said otherwise.

In many ways, I ran away from the pain of my father's death instead of entering into it. I denied that his death was going to happen soon, choosing to believe there was plenty of time. I left many of the details related to my father at the end to my sister. Even though I traveled six hours to be with him for his final lung cancer surgery and went again over the Fourth of July holiday to say goodbye—and was grateful he waited for me to get there on the night he died—I was not there with him in his last week of life. You could say I missed his closing summary, his last hurrah, a time that is very sacred. I continued with my "very important church work" and thought I had plenty of time to see Dad later. I regret missing his final week.

Years later, I looked at this weakness—along with others—as I learned more than I ever wanted to know about myself through the Enneagram, an insightful personality assessment tool. Out of all the various personality tests I have used during the years, the Enneagram is definitely the one that has helped me the most; it uncovers why people do what they do and how they tend to relate to the world. It has given me so many important insights into personality differences in my family, in the two staffs I have worked with over the years, and with my friends. I find it an invaluable tool in growing spiritually.

My father's death was not only painful because of the tremendous loss involved but also because it invited me to see that I was not in charge—had never been in charge. I could not and would not ever be able to control the timing of events; they don't work around my schedule. But God is good. As often happens with loved ones, about a week after Dad died, he appeared to me in a dream. He was young and healthy and happy, and we had a few moments of joy at our reunion. It seems that God knows when something is unfinished, and God steps right in to take care of us. I needed that.

Charging Ahead in Turbulent Waters

For the most part, I thrived in the role as bridge-builder to the congregation. I had done this for Mark in some ways, but now I moved into it on a whole new level for Paul. Over the next few years—especially during campaigns of one sort or another—I arranged lunches between leaders and Paul. I was there also, and these initiatives worked well. Paul understood that I liked to communicate, and he made sure that he was available to me. He was a good listener.

Paul was also a good preacher with a laid-back kind of delivery—didn't say a lot but you listened when he did speak. He also had his own kind of humor that took me a while to embrace—the kind of inside humor that some men use to bond with other men—in a playful way. I enjoyed his stories about the men's softball team at church—his friendship group. Someone was always sliding into third base or getting out at home, although Paul never made himself the hero. He showed his love and fondness for Maggie, his school-teacher wife, and spoke of her often, saying things like, "Maggie told me not to mention this, but…"

In general, he gained traction, and the transition seemed to be moving along nicely without problems until 1998, when Paul, in a desire to move the church forward, initiated a feasibility study concerning the future of the church.

At first, Paul's approach appeared to be a good one. The staff and committees would ease into the discussion about the church's future and how to best use the 17 acres just north of the church that we owned. An architectural firm was hired to conduct a feasibility study, and the firm suggested three options to grow the church: adding new construction to the existing campus, splitting the campus to include both the existing location and the 17 acres, or moving the entire operation to a 40-acre piece of property north of the church on Custer Road.

There were some good things about having options, but the disadvantage was that it divided us into two, maybe three camps. Paul was willing to let the congregation decide. But not me. I was confident. I thought it was always better to be as visionary as possible. Isn't that what God wanted and what the church had done to get where it was now? Why should we change our approach to something that might limit future growth? So, I charged ahead, believing that someone had to guide the congregation toward the visionary choice, the exciting choice. Surely God wanted us to remain the biggest United Methodist church around—to continue to lead the Plano region in growth. It was a good thing for the church that I knew the best way to move us forward!

Oh, dear. My competitive side and ego kicked in, but I did not see it. I was not ready to see any of my faults. I was too busy forging ahead, denying any problems with the plan I preferred. I was convinced the church should buy new land and construct a beautiful new campus. I had even seen 100 acres available on a key corner north of our location where significant expansion was expected, according to the official growth prospects. I was convinced that the thousands of new residents expected to move there in coming years would make great new members of our church community.

Forgetting that it is never good to get out ahead of the senior pastor, I made the mistake that associate pastors should never make. I worked diligently and passionately to encourage, inspire, and persuade the visionaries in our congregation to push for the most forward-thinking option. I was on a mission and was carrying them with me. The congregation had a light in their eyes as they went onward and upward, dreaming together. It was exciting, exhilarating.

Until the night the church voted. The sanctuary was filled to capacity—1,500 people. The entire youth group was there, along with Sunday School classes, small groups, all the staff, and others. I could hardly wait to hear the results. When the vote came back, it was to remain on our current campus. I was devastated—could not believe it. What was our church thinking?! Did we really want to settle for second best? How could Custer Road United Methodist Church choose to miss this incredible window of opportunity?

I wasn't the only person disappointed. A like-minded church member commented, "The other United Methodist churches in town are going to be thrilled with this decision." Three days later, Paul called me into his office. I was still smarting from the vote. He started gently, as he said something like, "The staff parish chair told me I needed to talk to you." Soon I realized he was reprimanding me for taking too firm a position, saying too much, and getting too involved in the entire process. He was reining me in.

I do not remember how I responded. I must have blocked it, for I was never prepared for bad news. Besides, how could I be wrong if my intentions were so good? I just wanted to help the church grow. Needless to say, I was not ready to apologize, and it took me a few years to realize that I needed to. I had charged ahead, confident that I had the best solution, and I did not want to see the problem I had partly created. I avoided listening to other ways of seeing our future.

I did not get what I wanted. It was the beginning of a humbling time for me, having to accept the fact that Paul brought a different style of leadership, and I needed to let go. It was a new day, and I was not in charge.

Now, more than 26 years later, I see how God has worked for good in the bigger picture and vision for Custer Road UMC. The church has thrived on its current campus and continues to grow and impact the community. However, when I drive by the corner several miles to the north where I had wanted to relocate, just for a moment, I see a church there. It's a United Methodist church with a steeple, and it's alive and thriving, reaching thousands of people hungry for what Custer Road UMC has to offer. Some dreams never die.

More Restlessness

Something inside of me changed after the night of the vote. I could not put it into words, but I was not the same. It was now fall of 1998. Custer Road UMC was doing well in so many ways, and there was much to be excited about. The respite program for parents of special education children was reaching new parents, and several of us had been on mission trips to Russia which was a great opportunity to build bridges. The Sunday School classes and small groups were thriving and growing. All of that was important to me because I was still in success mode.

However, I was restless once more, and I couldn't figure out why. I assumed the Spirit was nudging me to start something new, and I thought about teaching a new class or even going back to school and getting a Doctor of Ministry. That was what several of my friends did when there was a lull in their ministries, and it seemed to work for them.

Added to this restlessness was the fact that there seemed to be tension between one of the younger staff members and me. I did not like conflict, and Paul liked it even less. I had also learned from past mistakes that it was never a good idea to put a senior pastor in a position of needing to choose one staff member over another. Still, I wanted support from Paul and what I thought would help—more authority. "I need a more definite role, a supervisory role," I told him. He responded, "Not sure that is the answer, but it is important for you to know that I want you here as long as I am here. You are very valuable to me and to the church community."

I never became a supervisor, but I did receive a significant raise in January of 1999. I discovered that there was more than one way to address a concern! I was disappointed, but when I reflect on it, Paul did the right thing. I was not the supervisor type, and he valued me enough to give me a raise, which benefitted me more in the long run.

About this time, another important event was unfolding. In the spring of 1998, Reverend Stan Copeland came to a Dallas-area church, Lovers Lane UMC, to serve as its fourth senior pastor. The church was declining rapidly, and Stan was charged with the challenging and difficult task of bringing it back to life.

He appeared to be the kind of leader who would not be intimidated by this kind of challenge, and I made note of his ministry experience. I was curious about why he had been chosen for this kind of assignment in a large church. I found out that he was strong in evangelism, a good preacher, and was just 38 years old. He had helped start a new church out of First UMC Houston that involved purchasing a large tract of land on the west side of the city. It was the first such dual campus for a church in our denomination. (Stan has a Doctor of Ministry from United Theological Seminary that addressed church expansion like this.)

I Am Enough

Apart from his professional expertise, he had more life—and death—experience than just about anyone. While serving as an associate pastor for a church in East Texas, Stan was diagnosed with Leukemia at just 26 years of age. He received medical treatment in Houston where he had just accepted a position at First UMC Houston. Thanks to experimental drug treatments and God's grace, he was cured, but that singular experience would shape his life and his preaching forever.

In 1998, he was part of a network of senior pastors and associates of large United Methodist Churches from across the country. I was part of this group also, and Stan told me much later that when the Lovers Lane Staff-Parish Relations committee encouraged him to look for an executive pastor, he thought of me—although I was unaware of that at the time. On the surface, I appeared to have the strengths for the position, since I had served as the first woman chair of The North Texas UMC Conference Council on Finance and Administration.

More important to Stan was the fact that I enjoyed politics and had led the charge for Don Underwood—the pastor of a large United Methodist church in Plano—to be elected as a delegate to The United Methodist Church General Conference in 1996. As a result, Don went on to be elected in the next five conferences—2000, 2004, 2008, 2012, and 2016—before retiring. I appreciated the fact that Don had the wisdom to represent the local church well in what was sometimes a very bureaucratic United Methodist Church, and that like me, he believed in long-term pastorates and the stability they bring to a church.

In the summer of 1998, I ran into Stan at a church growth conference, and we had an important conversation. He got right to the point. "I would like you to consider coming on staff at Lovers Lane. I think you would be a good fit there."

I replied, "I appreciate you thinking of me, but I could never do that. I cannot imagine leaving Custer Road."

He responded, "You seem to love evangelism and growing the church, and you could write your ticket at Lovers Lane. It is going to be exciting as Lovers Lane rebuilds and begins new ministries and I know you thrive on challenges." Stan was making his case.

"Yes, but I have so many strong relationships at Custer Road that I have built over the years. I have roots there, and I love working with Paul Goodrich," I resisted.

Stan concluded, "We can talk again."

I was intrigued but not at all convinced. I knew that I was not particularly looking for a challenge; I had found my niche as a long-term associate in a large church and believed Custer Road UMC was the best place for that. I was known and loved there. The thought did occur to me, however, that I was now in my early 50s. Even though I was hoping to be in ministry for a long time, if I were ever going to make a move, now was probably the right time.

So, I began to consider it. I started listening. A few lay leaders made comments like, "You have high energy and are an entrepreneur." Another said, "You are a mover and a shaker." A colleague said, "You do not do well in a holding pattern." About this time, I read a devotion that said: "God's desire is to take you from where you are to where you want to be." It seemed I was getting a message.

The original Kilbourne (United) Methodist Church building where I attended Sunday School and worship as a child and later married Don. This building was torn down to make room for the current church building.

An early photograph, c.1955, of our annual family vacation to Colorado. My mom is resting her hands on Diane's shoulders, I stand in the middle, and my dad holds David in his arm.

Diane (left) and I (right) pose at a lookout point while on vacation in Colorado.

Don and I are married in the sanctuary of Kilbourne United Methodist Church on November 6, 1965, flanked by the bridal party with guests in attendance.

A 1988 article in the Plano Star Courier *reports on the changes that congregations experience when women enter the ministry. The story quotes me as its primary subject and features my headshot from the early days at Custer Road.*

The sanctuary of Custer Road United Methodist Church opened in 1990 and is oriented so the front door faces Custer Road, a design requirement specified by the building committee. When it was completed, the steeple was the tallest in town.

Bishop William B. Oden and I enter a packed house in the newly dedicated sanctuary of Custer Road United Methodist Church in the early 1990s.

The choir looks on as I give a sermon at Custer Road in the early 1990s.

Chapter Seven

When God Calls

I am about to do a new thing; now it springs forth, do you not see it?

—Isaiah 43:19

Obvious pride welled up in Aunt Bee as she told me more about David's career in Louisiana politics.

"He saw that our parish was not being represented well at the state level, and he wanted to help with that, which he did. He was good at being persuasive, gaining respect among his colleagues as he gave speeches to the Louisiana State Legislature as an elected representative from West Carroll Parish. He made $300 a year—we were not exactly rich."

"Did he have to campaign?" I asked Aunt Bee.

She replied, "Oh, yes. He delighted in interacting with people throughout the parish."

Aunt Bee seemed to be particularly pleased when she commented, "He was reelected three times. He was not a 'yes' man to the governor, Huey P. Long, and he believed in voting his conscience instead. He had lots of friends and was a gentleman in his relationship with colleagues and voters. If someone did not vote for him, it did not seem to bother him. In fact, when our house burned in the spring of 1939, many of his colleagues in the legislature, from all over the state—those who voted like him along with those who did not—sent money to help rebuild our home. Daddy hired a neighbor to oversee the project, paying him five dollars a day. That gives you some idea of the cost of living back then."

Fascinated, I kept up my barrage of questions, "I love the fact that he enjoyed the political world and had so many friends. I am curious; did he like to dress up like my dad does?"

"Oh, yes, he took great pride in his appearance. He wore a suit and tie every time he went to Oak Grove, which was often. He wore colorful ties and wanted Nannie to wear dresses with loud colors also."

I wondered if I could be like him.

A New Direction

I continued to struggle for a few more months, but in the fall of 1999, while walking with my friend, Cathy, in our neighborhood, I realized that my struggle was over. I blurted out to her, "I am going to do it. I am going to take the leap and make the move to Lovers Lane. I believe I will regret it if I don't." For the first time, I knew that God was saying to me it was time to let go and to graduate from the church I had served for almost 20 years—a church that had been my home, my anchor, my security, and my place to belong, a place that I had been so highly invested in for 20 years.

Cathy happened to be a member of Custer Road UMC, and she listened closely and did not try to talk me out of it. I was relieved when she understood.

Thankfully, Don didn't need any convincing. He was loved and cared for at Custer Road, but it was never his social world like it was mine. The conversation we had early on about maintaining our own distinct professional lives made all the difference, and he was going to support me no matter what decision I made. Wendi and Trey were also supportive. If I was going to make a life-changing decision, it seemed to be the right time to do so.

Once I came to peace about making the move, I still dreaded the idea of telling the congregation. Even worse than that was telling Paul. I wanted so much to honor our ministry together, the healthy working relationship we had, and our strong mutual commitment to Custer Road, so I practiced what I would say. And I prayed a lot.

As I prepared to talk to Paul, I thought of what I had said to my district superintendent, "I am ready to begin my second half of ministry, to move into a new environment, to lead in a new way, to embrace new challenges." In many ways, I felt like a missionary called to a new place to share what I knew. No matter that the new place may not be asking for that, and that I had no idea what I was getting into.

In early January 2000, God gave me what I considered to be the right opening to connect with Paul. It was not only the beginning of a new year, but the beginning of a new decade and a new millennium. Things were going well at Custer Road, and he was feeling confident about the church and his leadership. It was a good time to talk.

I took a deep breath and began. "I've just had my annual conversation with the district superintendent. We talked about how well Custer Road is doing. She (yes, we had a female district superintendent!) ended by bringing up my professional future, reminding me that if I ever wanted to do anything different, now was the time."

Paul emphasized that it would be my decision to make, and again, he stated that he would love for me to stay. I thanked him and explained that having reached this stage, I believed the time had come for me to make a move. "I don't know what I would have done without you in so many areas," Paul responded, easing my worries.

I was relieved, for I did not want to hurt him or the congregation in any way. Once again, he had come through. He promised we would stay connected and help one another through the transition and beyond. Then I left the meeting, all the while thanking God that we could work together to make the steps ahead positive for all involved. I knew it was a significant ending for me, and I wanted it to be a good ending for both of us and for the congregation. It felt right.

In the coming days, Paul kept his promise, and I kept mine. He bragged on me to the staff and to the congregation. I bragged on him. We had good conversations about the future, and he gave me good advice. He did not distance from me or treat me any differently than before I made the decision. In other words, he was a good friend. He gave me the blessing and the closure that I needed and had not gotten in the past. His affirming words helped heal me from pain I had not been willing to look at before. Mark's abrupt departure had been difficult for me and for the congregation, but this was a moment of redemption. As a result, my friendship with Paul remains strong today.

The year 2000 was pivotal for me on so many different levels. On a professional level, I embraced both my goodbye party at Custer Road UMC and my warm welcome at Lovers Lane UMC. The sadness I felt in leaving was tempered by the excitement I felt at what could be coming next.

At the goodbye party, I looked around the room and thought first of my family. We'd been through so much together since I had first dared to enter seminary. Wendi and her husband Bryan were giddy in expectation of our first grandchild. (I love reminding that granddaughter today about this part of our family story.) Trey was talking with some of his youth group members, a few of whom have remained lifelong friends. Don looked proud. My mom was enjoying it all, celebrating with me and taking lots of pictures.

My family and a few other friends in the room were the people I loved most in the world. My friend, Camille, had helped me choose what to wear that day, and other friends said, "I can't believe you are leaving us, but I know it will be good for you." Here they all were, blessing me to go out and begin this new journey.

I had cried often up to that moment, remembering, even savoring, moments from the early days at Custer Road: the first office in the portable building with Mark, worshiping in the school and setting up the chairs every Sunday, the first building, constructing the education building, starting all those classes from scratch. Memories of worshiping in the stunningly beautiful new sanctuary flooded my mind.

We were constantly making room for new people in those days. I enjoyed the large youth choir singing every Sunday, leading Wednesday night Bible studies and Stephen Ministry, traveling on mission trips, making mistakes, being forgiven, teaching the Experiencing God class four times that solidified my relationship with a real and personal God, developing friendships with good colleagues and with so many lay leaders. I did not want to worry about the future, but I was realizing that the future was here.

The year 2000 was significant on a personal level as well. Don's and my first grandchild, Hailey Brooke Sanchez, was born September 12, 2000, and was later baptized at Lovers Lane UMC. Five other grandchildren—Pierce, Kamryn, Landry, Hayden, and Drake—were all baptized there in the next two decades. Trey moved out of our home in July 2000, after graduating from Baylor University. He then landed his first job in Richardson, Texas, close to our home; a Custer Road friend, Debbie Mrazek, helped him get that first employment opportunity. And I bought a new car for the first time in nine years.

One of my friends put it this way, "You are going to Lovers Lane UMC, hitting the accelerator, and getting in the fast lane." He was right; the pace of my life was about to pick up as one millennium ended and another began—a major transition time in a major transition year.

Adjusting and Adapting

In the early 1940s, northwest Dallas was still dotted by acres of empty pastures and fields. Anticipating rapid residential development in the area, the Dallas District Extension Board of the Methodist Church decided to purchase two lots in the 5000 block of West Lovers Lane—property for a future church.

With World War II in full swing and building materials in short supply, the first meeting of Lovers Lane UMC was held in a small, rented house at 3924 Parkside Drive on February 4, 1945. Tom Shipp, an associate pastor at Highland Park UMC, was assigned to the new congregation and brought 18 couples with him to kick things off. By 1946, the fledgling congregation had outgrown the rent house and began meeting at John S. Bradfield Elementary School. Later that year, when Wallace Chapel was completed, the congregation immediately outgrew it. Unable to expand any further on the land or build a steeple due to flight paths coming in and out of nearby Love Field, the congregation found a permanent home at Northwest Highway and Inwood Road in 1960 and celebrated the groundbreaking on its present facility in 1970.

The rapid growth of Lovers Lane UMC beginning in the 1940s mirrored much of the growth we enjoyed at Custer Road UMC in the 1980s. But by the time I arrived on campus, Lovers Lane was in a completely different stage of life. I didn't know it then, but I would need to make adjustments, *major* adjustments. Lovers Lane would challenge me to reevaluate the assumptions I brought to ministry and to church growth in this more established and mature setting, and the transition wasn't going to be easy.

One thing is for sure, I was never bored at Lovers Lane UMC—not even for a moment. Stan's style of leadership pushed the envelope on every level. The church was always on the move with one initiative after another—starting the Alpha course (a popular study program on what it means to be a Christian), training the leadership, conducting a capital campaign, building a new Family Life Center. For the most part, I enjoyed being right in the middle of it all—lots of activity. I was in my comfort zone again.

When I attended a church growth conference shortly after arriving at Lovers Lane UMC, Lyle Schaller, a parish consultant, commented, "Women in their 50s are the best asset the church has today." Since I was now 53, I loved that statement and was ready to do my part to prove it true. Maybe it was a lofty goal, but soon I believed that I was in the right environment and with the right colleague to help carry it out.

Of course, nothing went as I expected. I wanted to be seen as a church growth expert who had all the answers, but Lovers Lane was not even asking those kinds of questions. The staff was wonderful to me but not impressed at all with all my suburban church statistics or my passion for church growth.

The congregations were very different. I'd expected lots of children and young families. Instead, I found many singles and older adults. I'd expected the staff to be small and centered around what I considered the basics—worship and Sunday School. Instead, the staff was large and driven by mission, outreach, and pastoral care. I was dismayed when I learned that the church prioritized giving to the community over ending the year in the black. While I admired the church's generosity, I believed that its financial strategy was just not sustainable. I'd been hired—I thought—to manage such things, to put on my administrative hat and teach everyone about healthy priorities, running a church, and operating with a much smaller staff. Once again, I was mistaken.

I got my first glimpse that this approach might not work well at the first staff retreat. Stan began to talk about his vision for the fall that would include mission events, new weeknight programs, and invited speakers for Sunday mornings in September while he would be out of town. I blurted out some type of question like, "Shouldn't the church focus on the basics and spiritual things on Sunday mornings?"

It was not one of my best moments, and the staff responded to this by saying things like "We trust you, Stan" and "Stan has been here long enough to decide." Needless to say, I felt awful!

Later, Stan's secretary asked me, "Do you still want to come?"

I replied, "It is going to be an adjustment."

She responded, "My pastor (from another local United Methodist church) told me to be patient with you."

For the first time I could laugh at myself, and that helped me take a step back and gain a little perspective. I needed to slow down, exhale, and ease my way into this new community—not come rushing in like a windstorm and expect everyone to follow my lead.

The next day at the retreat the staff was extra friendly, asking me for advice on their ministries. At the closing when we were to say what we were thankful for, I commented, "I am thankful for all that Lovers Lane UMC is doing and for Stan's leadership in the conference." Before we left, he mentioned that he was not going to invite all those outside speakers for Sunday mornings in September.

I had many adjustments to make. The biggest one in the first few months was worship. Everything felt a little off. I didn't realize how traditional and suburban I was, but I did know that I had been very comfortable in the sanctuary at Custer Road UMC with its center aisle, beautiful communion table, and cross right in the center. The seats at Custer Road were arranged in a semi-circle so that everything felt close, even intimate. The choir stood front and center, leading the congregation.

The sanctuary at Lovers Lane was beautiful, but in a very different way. In time, I grew to love the stained-glass

I Am Enough

windows with incredibly vibrant colors symbolizing the Holy Spirit moving up toward the cross. I struggled early on, however, with connecting to the congregation since the altar table was so far away. The contemporary sanctuary had no center aisle, and the choir was seated in the gallery in the back of the large room.

My discomfort—maybe grief—showed up in two or three anxiety attacks that I experienced the first few weeks while leading worship. Everyone seemed to ignore them, but I knew I was not myself. I went to a therapist who said, "Take a deep breath and remind yourself that you can move past your fear."

I also struggled with my role in worship. I wanted to be a leader from the beginning, doing what I had done at Custer Road UMC—greeting, praying, connecting with everyone. However, there were lots of staff, many more than we had at Custer Road, and they assumed many responsibilities that I was eager to take upon myself. I realized I needed to be patient—which was hard for me. Relaxing, when I could think of so many things to be worried about, proved a real challenge for my Type A personality.

Some of the best advice came from Paul. He told me, "Don't be interested in a title or a big sign on your door announcing how important you are, for that is the wrong message to give." He added, "The biggest challenge will not be with the congregation; it will be with the staff." He was right. The congregation welcomed me with open arms.

The staff, too, was open and welcoming, but since there was still so much change in the air with Stan coming in as senior pastor, no one had really landed in their roles, and everyone seemed to be on hold. Stan was a strong leader and an outstanding preacher; in fact, he's the best week in and week out preacher in the pulpit that I have ever heard, but management of staff and lay teams was not his thing.

He would cast the vision and assume the staff could be self-sufficient and figure things out as they went along, leaving a lot of room for different ways of seeing things. He had high expectations, and while he wanted to be involved in almost every administrative decision, his perfectionistic side made him slow to pull the trigger—another adjustment.

Stan's confidant on the staff—Dudley Dancer—helped me by saying, "Don't wait on Stan to bless things. Just go ahead and do what you do best."

Digging In

I did what Dudley said and got back on track. I started a new Sunday School class—my favorite thing to do—for young couples, inviting new couples when they visited worship. I also started teaching a Women's Prayer Fellowship that became a great way of reaching new women.

Stan and I worked to find the right balance working together, and I had to learn to trust his timing. Despite his patient nature, he loved my excitement and encouragement for his vision and his far-reaching dreams for the church—even if he didn't always want suggestions from me on how to get there. He would get there—in his own way. He was confident. But I was confident, too. My colleague Dudley Dancer said that watching the two of us was like watching a boxing match as we duked it out at times.

"I think the church should start a new worship service on Thursday nights," Stan suggested.

"Why doesn't the church take that time and energy to strengthen Sunday morning first?" I responded.

Stan didn't mind my outspokenness, and he said he wanted honest feedback. I soon learned to pray for the right timing. He often said that he felt responsible for helping me succeed; he felt guilty about a music minister he had chosen who ended up leaving because of problems with the staff, and he did not want me to make the same mistakes. (I seemed to find different ones to make.) Together we developed a kind of sister/brother type of friendship that worked for the most part.

It took me awhile to see that he was hard first on himself and then on those he was closest to. He was a perfectionist in many ways. Since I had not had that kind of challenge and feedback from a colleague before, I hadn't realized I needed it. Stan pushed me to get better at everything I was doing and was invested in me. Gradually—very gradually—I learned to listen to him.

"You often get in a hurry to get a task done, and just want to finish it instead of doing it right. You are so eager to recruit someone that you ask the first person you see," Stan commented.

"Umm," I responded, hating the feeling of being critiqued. "You may be right." I suggested to him, "Can't you ever tell someone 'No?' You take on way too many projects."

He replied, "I enjoy—almost have to have—several projects going on at one time. That is the way I am wired, and I have the personality profile that shows that." (He was referring to his Birkman Lifestyle Grid.)

Bill Hinson, Stan's mentor at First UMC Houston, had been hard on him, holding him to a high standard, and Stan had—for the most part—come through for him. We both shared glory days in our former churches where we were helping bring in hundreds of members a year, and it was hard for us to acknowledge that those days were over.

Neither of us, however, lost faith in what Lovers Lane UMC could become. Three months after I'd started my position, Stan said, with a great deal of confidence, "20 years from now we'll look back and see August 2000 as a turning point at Lovers Lane." That came true, but not in the way we both assumed. God had bigger and better dreams for Lovers

Lane than just growing the numbers of people, as I was to see in time.

About six months after I arrived, Stan had an important decision to make about his own future. He was being pursued by First United Methodist Church in Houston, where he had served for seven years as an associate pastor, to become their senior pastor. He had a deep love for that church, and he knew the church well. I knew this was going to be a hard decision for him and was very relieved when he decided that the timing was not right, but it was a reminder of how quickly things could change—especially in The United Methodist Church system.

Stan's decision to stay was an important one—first for the church and second for the staff and for me. His reputation as the best preacher in the Dallas area was established by now, and his radio audience on WRR-FM (101.1 FM)—*the* Dallas station on Sunday mornings, broadcasting local church services—was increasing every week. I also knew that there were going to be several challenges ahead, and I was certain that the church needed Stan's visionary leadership to go forward. He was expanding my understanding of what church was all about, teaching me that meaningful visions for a church were as much about the kinds of people the vision attracted as the numbers of people sitting in a worship service. Big conversion.

My second conversion at Lovers Lane happened when I realized how important it is to have diversity in a healthy congregation. I started taking a fresh look at my approach to starting new groups and classes. I saw that starting groups formed around affinity and everyone looking alike may not be the best way after all.

By 2004, I had a decision of my own to make. Rev. Jim Dorff, my district superintendent, asked me to accept an appointment to become the senior pastor at First UMC Frisco, which was a vibrant and growing church and a good match for me in many ways. While I had not asked for a change and was surprised by the invitation, I knew it was an incredible opportunity; he was giving me the chance to be a senior pastor, the pastor in charge. I could do this job as a woman and pave the way for more women in the future, and that part was appealing to me.

Unfortunately, I had only a few days to pray about the decision. I struggled, but I could not come to peace about moving. I would like to say that God spoke clearly, telling me what to do, but it was not that simple. I believed that God would work in either place, and I did not fear that one decision was good while the other one was bad.

I believed that my ministry was not finished at Lovers Lane; in fact, I believed I was just getting started. I knew I could make a long-term positive impact there as an associate, and I also felt that I needed the kind of growth in my soul

I Am Enough

that was happening there. So, I declined the offer and chose to stay, confident that God would open new doors in the future. I did not have long to wait.

Chapter Eight

Growing Up

It takes courage to grow up and turn out to be who you really are.
—E. E. Cummings

Rethinking My View of Church
For many years I thought that the church existed mainly for nice respectable people wanting to become nicer and more respected. It was a good place to make friends and to have fellowship with other people like me. But I began to question that. Could it be about something deeper and more life-changing? Could it be about repentance, forgiveness, and taking large leaps of faith? Could it involve embracing differences rather than reinforcing my own ways of thinking? I was about to find out.

Soon after arriving on the Lovers Lane UMC campus, I discovered that something more than the usual church stuff was happening in the house across the street from the church.

The Center for Spiritual Development—focused on the Twelve Step Ministry—stood in a rather private area facing Northwest Highway. Owned by the church and specially zoned for church use, this ministry was known throughout the community, not only because of the important spiritual work being done there, but also because it was located very near the one-time home of Tom Landry, the popular coach of the Dallas Cowboys.

It was not connected to the rest of the Lovers Lane UMC campus and seemed to be a rather inconspicuous, mysterious, and even secretive place. Cars came and went during all hours of the day as people from across North Texas—who mostly wanted to remain anonymous—came to get support. It was not your usual church crowd and certainly not the typical North Dallas crowd. I think that was the reason I was so drawn to it.

When I visited an open meeting of the Twelve Step Ministry located in the Center, I was blown away by the transparency and humility of the members. I found a place where people were honest, open, and truthful about the problems in their lives and the pain caused not only to themselves but also to their families. It was a place where people sought real life change, believing that change could and must happen.

Wow…this group not only had problems; they openly admitted it. "My name is Joe, and I am an alcoholic." Unlike most of us, they were aware enough to know that they were in over their heads with something that was bigger than themselves, and they needed help from a "power greater than themselves." I found their humility and authenticity to be genuine, fierce, and inspiring. They had found a sanctuary of their own, and most of them left the weekly meetings partially healed and resilient enough to make it to the next meeting.

I began to wonder why so many life changes were happening over there—outside the church—instead of inside it. Inside the church, people seemed to be talking about sin as something foreign to them, reserved for a few weak moments or a few people who rebelled or acted out. They didn't seem to feel a sense of urgency about making lifestyle changes or forming better habits.

Instead, most church people tended to feel sorry for these "poor people across the street" and saw them as different from people like themselves. At first, I, too, kept my distance and did not connect with many of them. But God was on the move, and a breakthrough occurred in the first new member class at Lovers Lane UMC that I helped teach. When I asked everyone to introduce themselves and say something about who they were, most said that they had been invited by a friend or had found the church by driving by. Then one of the men quietly said, "I'm Bill, and I am an alcoholic."

You could have heard a pin drop! The whole atmosphere of the class changed after that. Everyone who spoke after Bill not only told their name but shared something they were struggling with in their life or in their family. It was as if a breath of fresh air had just blown through the room, and the group became more real, more transparent. The ice was broken; the façade that we were all living the perfect life was gone. In fact, thanks to Bill, the distance between us seemed to disappear.

I remembered that this tell-it-like-it-is attitude had been a part of Lovers Lane church since its beginning. In the early days, Tom Shipp, the first pastor, had welcomed and trusted everyone alike, inviting them to worship, including alcoholics, many of whom became ushers. Today, more than 75 years later, weekly groups meet at the Center to provide support not only for alcoholics, but also for people suffering from addictions of all kinds—gambling, heroin, nicotine, cocaine, eating disorders, opiates, internet and technology, online gaming, and yes, even sex and love addictions. The director, Andrea Tabor, told me that when they began groups for more hard-core addictions, the numbers rapidly increased because there was such a need for a safe place where people in the community could share openly about their pain and desire to change.

I was curious about what could keep someone coming to meetings like this week after week, day after day. I thought of

Jesus' question, "Do you want to get well?" (John 5:6 NIV) These people seemed to be saying "Yes!" They were reminders that getting well is all about surrender, humility, and the willingness to change. It seems that the hardest part is the first step, acknowledgment of the human flaw—powerlessness to get well on our own. In the words of singer, songwriter Mac Davis, "Lord, it's hard to be humble when you're perfect in every way."

I began to reflect on my own life. I was flooded with questions. Had I been afraid to look inward? Did I still tend to stay with the status quo rather than desire a deeper change? Was I in touch with my flaws, my weaknesses, my strong desire to be right? What did it mean to be a real and genuine Christian? As you've probably guessed, God was moving in my life.

Church Combat and Learning to Apologize

After the ups and downs of the first few years, I seemed to settle in and find my niche on the staff at Lovers Lane UMC. There were some good moments, but there were also challenging times. In fact, 2005 brought unrest and turmoil. And much to my dismay, I was caught right in the middle of it with no place to hide.

The music director, who was hired quickly because of her expertise with secular music, was leading a large choir at Lovers Lane and took great pride in being excellent in many ways. She was also restless and eager to have more decision-making power.

After rolling out a new initiative for the staff, Stan took a much-deserved sabbatical in June of 2005, and I was left in charge. I wanted the leadership role and was confident I could do it well, but when I experienced tension with the music staff, the conflict spread rapidly, leading to a very painful time for the staff, the choir, and parts of the congregation.

I had navigated disagreements before, but I was about to learn what hardball church politics really looked like.

When the choir director, along with her assistant she had recently hired, did not get their way about a hire they wanted to make, they began a highly organized attack on Stan and me, using emails to stir up as many disgruntled members as they could, especially in the choir.

The situation became so serious that Stan had to return from his sabbatical early. It was a pivotal time in my relationship with the church and with Stan as my Senior Pastor. With so many attacks coming at us, we were tempted to blame each other and to let our fear come out in unhealthy ways. For the most part, however, we rose above that. At times Stan showed sympathy and compassion for the role I played, saying, "You had to be me without me, and you were the one who made it possible for me to leave." At other times, he was aware of possible serious consequences, and in August of that year, as we battled our way through the conflict, he said, "I could lose my job over this."

Jim Gibbs, a key lay leader, wrote Stan a note on August 4 of that summer saying, "90 percent of us support you 110 percent. I will take care of you and let others know that I am a 'Stan-Man.'" In fact, never before had the key lay people of Lovers Lane come through so strongly and consistently. They were tough, patient, and available—stepping up when we needed them the most.

Two of our lay leaders—Frank Jackson and Dan Garner—worked tirelessly as peacemakers. They met one-on-one with some of the choir members and with others who were considering leaving the church, listening and trying to bring about healing. At the end of the day, the turmoil resulted in the loss of most of the choir.

I was struggling to find peace with the situation, and I was still in denial about any damage my decisions in the matter had caused. It took me months to apologize. I initially considered myself free of guilt because from my perspective, I was merely doing what I thought was best for the church. I had the backing of leadership. I had good intentions. Does this sound familiar? Unlike me, Stan had been meeting with people one-on-one and listening to how they felt. He asked me one day, "When are you going to apologize?"

With Stan's encouragement, I made one of the hardest pastoral visits I have ever made. It was to a couple, faithful choir members who had been there 20 years before me. They received me warmly as I said—and meant—the words, "I am sorry. I could have handled this differently." I did the same thing with a few others, and with each apology came a healthy dose of humility.

Why had it taken me so long to admit I was partly to blame? Could it be that I was like the people across the street—that in fact I also was addicted—addicted to being right? And unlike them, maybe I had been too proud to take an honest look at my part in the problem. Why had I been so afraid of dealing with the pain—of surrendering control to a greater power, fully embracing the power of the Holy Spirit at work in my life?

As I look back on those visits and that time in my ministry, I realize that something was shifting. Finally, I had "come to the end of myself" and let go of my ego long enough to own my part and to admit that I could have made a mistake. Maybe there had been a better way of handling the conflict. Like most people, it took pain and suffering to unsettle me enough to get me to pause, go deeper, and take a new look at the circumstances.

I later realized that my whole experience was what the Twelve Step Ministry and Alcoholics Anonymous call Step Eight: "Make a list of all people I have harmed and become willing to make amends to them all." It does not say: "Make a list of people who have harmed *me*." That is so much easier!

Growing Up

Making a list of people that have been harmed BY me and then genuinely apologizing is not for the weak of spirit. I see why some people take several years to do it.

I also see that people who want to grow spiritually must take initiative, acknowledge responsibility for their part of a problem, and then change their behavior going forward. It requires deep, difficult effort. I knew it was a step in the right direction for me—a step I needed to take, one of the hardest things I have ever done. Richard Rohr puts it this way, "Fortunately God reveals our sins to us gradually, so that we can absorb what we have done over time." Thank you, God, for taking it slow with me.

The Sky Clears
Another important event for the church occurred in fall 2005, the same year as the unrest and attacks. A member of the church, Margaret Folsom, told Stan that she was ready to donate two million dollars to build the long-awaited Shipp Chapel. She loved Stan, and she loved the church. It was a real vote of confidence in his long-term leadership there, and it jump-started our next capital campaign.

Stan's preaching—which had always been strong—rose to a new level. He was inspiring as he preached about the church being united as the Body of Christ; every event or worship service seemed to have added depth because of the pain the congregation had been through. I knew that I was changed, and many of the lay leaders were also.

Lovers Lane UMC was coming out of its stormy season and waking up to its full potential. That fall the church faced several financial challenges as it moved toward the end of the year. I was encouraged as the church took them one at a time and in the right order—first raising major money for Hurricane Katrina victims, then raising money to pay for all of our end-of-year local and global missional giving, and finally—*finally*—raising money to end our operational year in the black.

Stan gave me more credit than I deserved when he emailed the staff in January 2006, saying, "Donna raised over and above money by leading a quiet campaign behind the scenes with a group of six to eight people. It was the best December the church has ever had in Lovers Lane's history."

I finally understood. I was getting credit, but it was not about me. It was about what happens in the Body of Christ when God is moving. There were many years to come when Lovers Lane faced similar kinds of financial challenges at the end of the year, and every year was different. It did not always turn out like I hoped, but I never again doubted that it was God out front leading us, inspiring us to remember our abundance, and challenging us to respond to His incredible love for us. We were blessed.

Lovers Lane, which was beginning to feel like a family again, ended 2005 in a remarkable way, but of course, that did not resolve everything. There were more painful conversations, and members of the choir continued to leave. On the horizon, however, was Jimmy Emery, who arrived in 2006. In my opinion, he became the most gifted, most spiritual, and most loyal director of music that Lovers Lane UMC could have ever hoped to have. I never doubted for a moment that it was God who had sent him to us.

My colleague, Don Underwood remarked, "Lovers Lane is beginning a new era." Indeed, we were! Out of the discord, the pain, the suffering, the apologies, and the forgiveness had come spiritual growth, and best of all, more dependence on God.

Claiming Our Past: Loving All

Tom Bandy, a church-growth consultant, visited our campus in early 2005 to meet with church leaders and staff. He concluded his talk with a reminder about the church's ministry and mission potential by stating, "You will either become bottom-line-oriented or radically generous in your giving as a congregation."

I never forgot that statement from him. In the coming years the church moved toward being who it was uniquely called to be—sometimes thriving, sometimes struggling. In the end, however, the congregation became radically generous, and that has made all the difference.

Lovers Lane UMC is known in the broader Dallas community for being outwardly oriented, inclusive, and caring about the community, but most of all, for being authentic and real. I credit the church's first full-time pastor, Tom Shipp, for giving the church that identity from the beginning. As an orphan in his teenage years, Tom found grace, acceptance, and financial support in the Methodist church, and he never forgot it. He passionately wanted everyone else to experience that kind of acceptance and respect. Under his leadership, the 1954 building committee included three women—highly unusual in an institutional church at that time. Other women in the church also gladly served the African American community in Dallas by teaching Vacation Bible School in the African American neighborhoods in the 1960s.

This radical acceptance—this DNA—continued to be lived out through the years that Don Benton and Bill Bryan were pastors. The United Methodist Women seemed to lead the way, not only being out in the community and tutoring students at some of the elementary schools but also, in later years, taking trips to the southern border to see the plight of the immigrants. Lovers Lane continued to become the place to be when it came to addressing racism or defending other groups who were left out. I smiled, watching one group or another showing up at the church, thinking how happy Tom Shipp would be. His spirit was alive and well there—and Stan and the other pastors built on this legacy.

After Stan arrived in 1998, he led efforts to start a prison ministry, an African Fellowship, and a Zimbabwean Fellowship. A special needs ministry came soon after. The church's long-range planning team added the word "all" to our mission statement so that it stated and now reads, "Loving ALL people into relationship with Jesus Christ."

The Deaf Ministry began in 1999 when a young adult class that was very diverse had the idea of interpreting worship services for the deaf. Stan embraced this initiative, and Tom Hudspeth was appointed to lead the ministry. Charlotte Winters—who was on her knees praying for a place to serve the deaf when the call from Lovers Lane UMC came—became the first interpreter.

This young adult class included a disabled person, a person with a brain injury, persons from Russia and the Philippines, and a deaf person. It was a sign of things to come. Today, the deaf ministry at Lovers Lane UMC includes deaf lay servants, life groups, retreats, mission trips, American Sign Language classes, and connections with the worldwide deaf community in nine different countries.

"We have gone global," one of the young adults signed to me. "And my life has been changed by finding a church community that I feel I belong in."

It was no surprise, then, that during the 2008 Annual Conference, Lovers Lane UMC was recognized for having the largest number of professions of faith in the conference. Growth was not coming so much from other United Methodist churches as it was from people who were coming to faith for the first time. It was good news for the church since I knew by then that new people coming into the Body of Christ brought us a fresh message from God, often about our future. I was learning to pay attention.

Confronting Stereotypes
Paul Young, author of *The Shack*, arrived on the scene in 2009 and made a profound impact on the Lovers Lane UMC congregation, and on me. He spoke forcefully and clearly about the church being a healing place for all. His edgy novel featured God as an African American woman, Jesus as a man from the Middle East, and the Holy Spirit as Asian.

I loved, loved, his courageous attempts to confront the stereotypes that had long limited the work of most churches, keeping all of us in a smaller world. I found that I was no longer envying my friends who were in churches where everyone thought and looked alike. I knew I wanted and needed the challenge of different points of view. I also knew that I did not want to be limited to traditional ways of viewing God. I was grateful that God could also be seen, as Paul Young said, "…through the Holy Spirit, in art, or music, in silence, through people, in Creation, or in joy and sorrow." (William P. Young, *The Shack* [Windblown Media, 2007], 198).

Young's book and presentation were breakthrough moments for me in other ways. For the first time, I understood the personal part of the Trinity. He portrayed the three persons as a package deal who are equal, who are very comfortable with each other and who share life experiences with one another. I think one of my lifelong biases had been that God was a little more important than Jesus or the Holy Spirit, but Young made it clear this way of thinking was not true. When Mack, the main character of his book, asks, "Which one of you is God?" all three of them say together, "I am."

It is important to note that it was a Jewish friend of Tom Shipp, Pollard Simon, who helped endow the sanctuary at Lovers Lane UMC, and it was a gangster, Benny Binion, who sold the original land on Northwest Highway to the church. (Benny later moved to Nevada where gambling was legal and established a successful casino in downtown Las Vegas, The Horseshoe Casino.) These people were not insiders to the church; they were outsiders, reminding us that God's love has no boundaries, no parameters, no limits. One of the reasons Tom Shipp was loved so much is that he understood that and lived it out.

Broken Yet Beautiful

Every time I go into the sanctuary at Lovers Lane, I am reminded of the incredible colors of the stained-glass windows and the people who worship there. As the Twelve Step Ministry reminds us, people are each "broken yet beautiful"—a powerful way to describe who we are and how God sees us.

In 2009, I found a note from a visitor who happened to be at our church on a weekday. He wrote, "It was good to be at your church. I am a bit of a rebel when it comes to organized religion, and I hate big empty buildings. But your church is a living, loving church, and almost all the time we were here, there were people coming and going to and from all kinds of activities. The most remarkable thing was that the people seemed to be from every walk of life and from pretty much every age and culture. I was very inspired by this and am rethinking my view of church."

Yes! Once again, an outsider had spoken; a stereotype had been broken. I did not know it earlier in my ministry, but this is the kind of church that I always wanted to be a part of, a place where walls are broken down, where fear and distrust do not reign, where differences are celebrated, where new horizons await to be explored. I was thankful for all this, but I was most grateful that the church was helping me to open my heart and soul in greater ways.

It did not take me long to see that this new kind of reflection and vulnerability brought not just joy and gratitude but also pain and difficulty. Not all walls are easily broken down—sometimes they implode on us. And our hearts, when they are opened, can ache as much as they invite us to celebrate. Did I really have the courage to look at some of my prejudices and biases I had avoided up to now? Did I really want to grow up and see parts of myself I had kept hidden? I was not sure.

Then, an image of my mom came to me, one I mentioned earlier. She was 17 years old and about to graduate from high school. She was out in that cotton field in Pioneer, Louisiana, when the principal came to her house to tell her dad—who did not think she needed to go to college—that he had a scholarship for her for 25 dollars a month. She put the bag of cotton down in the cotton patch and walked out, leaving the bag behind—and with that move, leaving behind anything that would keep her from going forward in her life, anything that would limit her future. She did not look back.

It was no longer hard for me to do the same thing.

Chapter Nine
Facing Difficult Truth

Healing may not be so much about getting better, as about letting go of everything that isn't you—all of the expectations, all of the beliefs—and becoming who you are.

—Rachel Naomi Remen

Uncovering My Biases

Since I was finally opening myself up, God started giving me insights.

Be careful what you ask for from God.

My goal was to be more vulnerable and to encourage vulnerability in conversations and in the spiritual growth classes I was teaching at Lovers Lane. I wanted to be open and honest about my blind spots and weed out any bias or prejudice that had been hidden from me.

I realized in seminary from my professors that no one is totally objective; everyone has biases or preconceived notions, and they acknowledged theirs. The problem is if people don't become aware of these biases, the biases stay hidden and then pop out when least expected. I thought that I was open-minded and not judgmental; I did not think I was prejudiced. Now I was seeing that I was like everyone else; I am definitely biased in certain areas. Part of my new decision was to take risks and become more self-aware.

I was already being primed to take that leap because Lovers Lane was inviting me to look at the flaws in myself that I had never acknowledged before when my ministry seemed to be about success after success.

So, I dove in, not knowing exactly how to swim in these new waters.

It was at the church on a cold December night that, without warning, I was tossed into the deep end of the proverbial pool.

I was participating in "Everybody's Christmas," an annual event at Lovers Lane UMC in which people from homeless shelters, ex-offenders, and women affected by domestic violence come to the church for worship, food, fellowship, and winter coats. The night began, and I was SO excited—

keyed up—in anticipation of the events ahead, and I watched the buses full of people roll in around 6:00 p.m.

As the night progressed, I walked into the communion service for ex-offenders in the chapel where one of our African pastors was saying Jesus' words, "I was hungry, and you gave me something to eat … I needed clothes and you clothed me … I was in prison, and you came to visit me." (Matthew 25:35-36 NIV) I couldn't believe it! All of this was going on around me right there—people were eating together, giving coats out, listening to each other's stories. Wasn't this what Jesus was just saying we must do?

Next came the worship service for everyone. I sat on the front row and did not want to miss any part of it.

Sitting next to me was a man who had recently gotten out of jail; his name was Cadillac. During our conversations before and after worship, he mentioned that he had recently been in a terrible car accident, but that God had saved him. He was so grateful, but was genuinely struggling, "I just don't see why God would save someone like me." I listened but did not want to give a trite answer as we pondered it together.

The event lasted about two hours, and as he boarded the bus to go home, I saw him again. He mentioned once more that he wished God would show him why He had allowed him to live. This time, I was ready to respond. "Maybe God wants you to be around to help people like me to see that everyone is alike, that all are equal in God's eyes, and that we very much need each other."

A light and hint of joy came into his eyes. He knew I meant it. What he did not know was that earlier that night as I was helping give out coats, I was convicted of a sense of pride and superiority. It hit me like a bolt of lightning that maybe because of a lack of experience with people like him, I had subtly hung on to the lie that I was somehow a little better than people who didn't look like me or act like me. Why couldn't they just get their life together? In those moments, I saw how very wrong I had been. How could I dare think I was somehow better than others? Cadillac and I were brothers and sisters in Christ—all on the same playing field, so much more alike than different.

Could this be what white privilege was all about? Had I spent most of my life imprisoned to a biased way of thinking and being? Was a part of me that had been hidden and ignored coming to light? I finally caught a glimpse of this truth, realizing that it was not the ex-offenders, people from the homeless shelters, or the victims of domestic violence who needed freedom; I was the one who needed it the most.

I thought about the fact that this kind of honesty, truthfulness, and self-awareness was going on all the time in the AA groups across the street, where people were getting real about their illusions, biases, addictions, and defensive behaviors and acknowledging that none of them work. It also happens on church mission trips where different kinds of people travel together and share work and life on a more personal level. It happens in worship when the congregation experiences the most important thing a church can offer—communion with the Holy Spirit. It happens in the church nursery and preschool as diversity becomes more a part—a beautiful part—of the community. It happens in classes and groups and home fellowships every time and every place where people become free enough to see the humanity in everyone.

That night was a moment of truth for me.

I remembered a recent conversation in our family when someone said, "One of my friends is upset because she is not pleased with the behavior of her son's girlfriend. She is hoping that her son goes to a different college than the girlfriend."

Another family member responded, "Isn't it interesting that we easily criticize others while seldom seeing our own flaws?"

How true, I thought. It is so much easier to look out at others' faults than to go inward and face our own. *Ouch*—that hit close to home.

Listening to My Body

Another step I decided to take in facing truth and getting real involved tuning in to what God was saying to me in unconventional ways. I began to discover how creative God can be in helping me face that part of myself which is out of balance and unhealthy in my body. It's another way to listen. Since I tended to stay in my head instead of paying attention to feelings, I was often out of touch with deeper emotions, especially negative ones like anger. After all, anger did not fit my image of myself as a good and nice Christian woman. An event occurred in 2009 that brought all this out in the open.

The staff was moving into new office space after the church built a new building. Stan would have the largest office as Sr. Pastor, a great space on the corner with a bathroom included. Making matters more interesting was the fact that the two offices next to Stan in the office suite were much larger than the ten or more other offices. If that were not enough, these large offices had great windows with wonderful views. Who doesn't love a great view!

I convinced myself that I deserved one of those two offices. (I know this is petty, but at this point in my journey, I am afraid it was a big deal.) Stan took me on a tour of the new construction when it was almost completed, going into great detail about how wonderful my new office was—but it was not the office I wanted. I was wise enough not to express my anger directly, but not wise enough to let it go. I was wrapped up in my ego, and let my anger take over, which was not only causing me mental and spiritual anguish, but it was affecting my health, too. I *deserved* the bigger office!

In hindsight, the office drama moved me toward humility, which I needed. The assignment was a practical one, putting businesspeople closer to Stan. (I had a wonderful view from my new office also, and I came to see in coming years the advantage of where I had been placed). I did not understand the benefits at first because I mixed up my ego with my capital S Self—the one God had called me to be, my *best* self.

Interestingly enough, about this time, I began to have health issues with my stomach.

After working with a dietician, I discovered that I was allergic to foods containing gluten and needed to avoid sugar and salt. All my life I had suffered from migraines, but I never dreamed that it had anything to do with what I was eating. I began to eat healthier foods and to pay more attention to what I ate. I also went to a chiropractor who used what is called muscle testing to teach me the foods I was allergic to, making a big difference in how I felt. When I took a chance and ate something that was not good for me, I got a headache. My brain seemed to be saying that I could eat whatever food I wanted, but if my body did not like it, it would let me know.

I was learning that emotions could impact my health, so I also worked with the chiropractor on what part of my body was holding on to an emotion. Soon I learned that I was holding on to—you guessed it—anger. This anger seemed to be stuck in the part of my body where I was the most vulnerable, and for me, it was my stomach. It was time to let go of it.

The most important truth for me in all of this was to realize that I had *never* really been in touch with deeper feelings, especially ones I was not comfortable with. As a seven on the Enneagram, I loved to experience things; in fact, I tend to go from one exciting experience to another, and I thought this was feeling, but it is not. It is a way of keeping my feelings on the surface.

The Enneagram taught me this; I mentioned my deep appreciation for it earlier. It is a model of human psychology and personality theory that is based on the idea that each person has a unique and innate personality structure, or "essence," that shapes the way they see the world and themselves.

The nine types of the Enneagram are divided into one of three centers of intelligence: Heart Types, Head Types, and Body Types.

Heart types (Types Two, Three, and Four) depend on their emotional intelligence to understand their own reactions and connections with others.

Head types (Types Five, Six, and Seven—*me!*) depend on their intellectual intelligence to make sense of things and navigate the world around them.

Facing Difficult Truth

Body types (Types Eight, Nine, and One) depend on their instinctual intelligence to follow their "gut" and respond to threats and opportunities.

Sevens are extroverted, optimistic, versatile, and spontaneous. Playful, high-spirited, and practical, they can also misapply their many talents, becoming over-extended, scattered, and undisciplined. They constantly seek new and exciting experiences, but they can become distracted and exhausted by staying on the go. They typically have problems with impatience and impulsiveness. At their best, they focus their talents on worthwhile goals, becoming appreciative, joyous, and satisfied.

I had been holding back deeper feelings—sadness, anger, even compassion, and empathy. It was eating away at my ability to be a good pastor, a good friend, a good human being. Often, I would get so interested in completing a task that I would dismiss or ignore deep feelings, convincing myself that I had to get the task done instead of being present to the people around me. This was becoming a big problem that was preventing me from being real and authentic. I needed to take deep breaths and allow both positive and negative feelings to come—making friends with them instead of dismissing them.

As I look back on this stage in my life, I realize that God was moving, speaking, and helping me, primarily by speaking through my body and through other people, including my regular internist. I had a deep desire to get healthy—in fact, I had a sense of urgency about it—and I was praying for healers, for people who had different kinds of wisdom that I could learn from. I trusted that God would send them to me, and that is exactly what happened.

Under the Waterfall
During the first months of 2010, I was dealing with my food allergies and digestive issues. I had lost weight and was unsettled, even depressed.

Others could see something was wrong. Stan suggested taking some time off to heal and get healthy again.

I realized I needed to get away, so I traveled with two women friends, Priscilla and Sharon, to Kauai, an island known as the healing island. Kauai is Hawaii's fourth largest island and is sometimes called the "Garden Island," which is an entirely accurate description. The oldest and northernmost island in the Hawaiian chain is draped in emerald valleys, sharp mountain spires and jagged cliffs aged by time and the elements. Centuries of growth have formed tropical rainforests, forking rivers and cascading waterfalls! Some parts of Kauai are only accessible by sea or air, revealing views beyond your imagination. More than just dramatic beauty, the island is home to a variety of outdoor activities.

We got massages, we ate healthy food, and we relaxed—big time. We did nothing but soak in the atmosphere. I was

Facing Difficult Truth

beginning to believe this "island of healing" would live up to its name.

I have always been enthralled with waterfalls—their beauty and their energy. When Priscilla mentioned to a neighbor in the condo where we were staying that we were looking for a secluded waterfall, the neighbor offered to show us the perfect spot. It was in a very private, wooded location where few people traveled. Just getting there was quite an adventure, and by the time we arrived, I was a little nervous, but even more, I was excited. I heard the water before I saw it, and it sounded powerful and breathtaking—an ideal place to find the renewal I was searching for.

Priscilla went into the water first, and I followed. The rocks were slippery, but soon I was under the waterfall, feeling the weight of it. The water enveloped me, and it was strangely calming. My nerves gave way to peace. I felt loved and embraced.

Something was happening that I had never felt—spiritually, emotionally, physically. What was going on under that waterfall? Who was in this place with me? Not just my friends. God was there!

I sensed His reassuring energy, inviting me to enter into a deeper kind of trust, a trust and connection that could take me to places I had not yet gone. I wanted that and knew I needed to get over any fears about my future. It was an intimate moment, a humbling moment, a deepening of my awareness of God. It felt like a cleansing, a renewal—a baptism of sorts. Was I ready to trust Him more, accept His love for me, and take another leap of faith? In that moment, under the power of the waterfall, I said, "Yes! Yes!" I yielded, surrendered, and finally let go—making room for the healing that God wanted to make happen. And even though I wasn't physically well just yet, I knew I was headed in the right direction.

It hit me suddenly; had I lost touch with the most important part—that God loved me as I was? Had I listened to the world too much? I did not need to be perfect! I did not need to accomplish more—to do anything more—to be successful in God's eyes. I realized that I had never needed to earn God's love. He created me in love and would always love me as I was. I just needed to embrace it—to accept His acceptance and unconditional love for me. I could approach Him boldly with confidence and with nothing separating me from his Presence. Nothing can keep me from His overwhelming, never-ending, reckless kind of love, just as the song says. Yes, He was there and always had been there with me in every moment. I was not alone and never would be. For the first time in my life, I felt on a deep level that I was enough!

When I returned to the condo later that day, I felt as if a load had been lifted from my shoulders. Much of the fear of physical problems or of the future went away. Everything seemed clearer and brighter, more beautiful—like the day in kindergarten when I wore glasses for the first time. I was waking up in a new way to the truth that I, along with everyone else, has flaws—but the more important part is that God knows this and embraces me and loves me *with* these flaws. God embraces my imperfections!

No longer would I get caught up in the lie the world tells me over and over again that God's love for me is conditional and that I have to do something or look a certain way or have a certain kind of status to earn it. That way of thinking and being was over. Our relationship could be real and authentic. I had finally made a connection with my soul.

At the end of the two weeks in Kauai, I did not want to leave the island that brought me to a new kind of spiritual place in my life. But when I did return home, I was different. No more insecurities or feeling less than. I was enough. I felt a newer, stronger connection to God and to nature. I wanted to spend more time with God alone, and I saw the everyday beauty around me that I had been missing. I noticed sunsets I had ignored; I felt the energy of trees and plants, saw the liveliness of butterflies, the beauty of red cardinals. The natural world became something to delight in, to connect with, and to be grateful for. There was no place where I could not be in the presence of God, for God was not just out there but also "in all, through all, and with all." (1 Corinthians 15:28)

And, incredibly, my stomach issues were gone.

I relaxed. I made space in my life to recognize the richness all around me. I was present to the Presence. People, *all* people, became beautiful to me. I noticed the light in their eyes and knew it was the doorway to their souls. I vowed to get healthier and quit running away from deep emotions like anger and grief, empathy and humility. I wanted the courage to name these emotions when I experienced them. I wanted to grow in my ability to feel connected with others, to serve, to be more compassionate, and to trust that God was sending me important messages all the time.

It was almost too good to be true, but it *was* true. God's Presence was there with me and advocating for me in that present moment, nudging me forward, inspiring me, giving me wisdom, and inviting me to love others. He was taking me to places I had never been—an adventure of the highest order. The future looked bright.

Inner World Gets Attention

The waterfall experience stayed with me, and the light of truth was continuously being switched on within me. It was painful to admit, but now I knew that much of the growth I had experienced in the first half of my life had really just fed the immature, judgmental, and insecure side of me. The perfection in love that John Wesley called me to was sidetracked by detours, distractions, and a need to feed my ego instead of enlarging my world. My ego took care of my small 's' self, while my larger and more mature self was eager to come out.

When my son, Trey, was two and entered his pre-school class for the first time, we had an important moment together—one that I will never forget. He said to me, "Mom, come stay with me awhile." It was a tender moment between the two of us; I caught a glimpse of his heart and his desire to connect. Now I wanted to say the same thing to the Holy Spirit. "Holy Spirit, come and stay with me awhile. I want to connect with You more. I need You to help me. I have much work to do."

I made a new decision. I vowed to take my life back after many years of caring too much about being noticed and affirmed—thinking too much about winning and being on top of my game and not enough about losing and struggling. I had focused on my outer world, while my inner world was clamoring for attention. I had blocked the very thing that I wanted the most—a good relationship and connection with God. This realization was painful and difficult to face. I was not who I wanted to be; I had a long journey ahead to be more real, more human, more faithful.

So, I put on my take-a-risk hat and chose courage over comfort. I wanted to acknowledge and get rid of the false, fake, surface-level stuff. I wanted to stop being guided by my need to be needed, to achieve, to control, to be first, and to judge. Instead, I wanted to go for the real more often, for the genuine, the peaceful, and the true deeper self, the unselfish self, the capital S Self. I wanted to grow my soul. I wanted to move out of the dark into the light, out of the false self into the true me. For the first time, I saw that in my desire to be the nice Christian who followed the rules, drove the right car, had the right office, ate the right foods, achieved the right numbers, and made the right amount of money, I was missing the main thing—being real and authentic.

I was so afraid of failing or making mistakes that I stayed on the surface and focused on myself and my achievements. In an effort to avoid dealing with anything unpleasant or negative, I avoided sad or angry feelings that needed to be explored. I had been going down the inauthentic path. In fact, almost everyone is.

No wonder Jesus came to turn everything upside down! People spend too much time following something other than God's ways.

I've learned much from Richard Rohr, a Franciscan priest and writer on spirituality. Rohr was ordained to the priesthood in the Roman Catholic Church in 1970, founded the New Jerusalem Community in Cincinnati in 1971, and the Center for Action and Contemplation in his current home of Albuquerque in 1987. In 2011, PBS called him "one of the most popular spirituality authors and speakers in the world." His notable works include *The Universal Christ*, *Falling*

Upward, and *Everything Belongs*. His spirituality is rooted in Christian mysticism and the perennial tradition. His work feeds my soul and the souls of tens of thousands of seekers around the world.

Rohr calls our habit of taking the wrong path "false programs for happiness." In trying to do things right and climb the outward ladder of success, we miss the greatest insight of all: the true path involves acknowledging that everyone is broken, yet beautiful. Everyone has flaws. We are all connected in this way. This kind of soul work can be unsettling, uncomfortable, and painful. John 8:32 reminds us, "The truth will set you free," but it doesn't mean it won't make you miserable first.

Chapter Ten

Stepping Out

Everything has beauty, but not everyone sees it.
—Unknown

Promised Land

I was waking up to a much-needed balance in my life, and in the summer of 2010, I found what I needed in East Texas: a patch of peaceful land a little more than an hour and a half from my Plano home where I could build my own version of a restorative space.

My awakening in Hawaii had unleased a new but not unfamiliar perspective on life. I rediscovered the beauty of what had been my country life as a child, and I began tuning into sunrises and sunsets and the plethora of plants, birds, insects, and animals around me.

It took me until I was in my 60s to finally see the beauty and wonder of the natural world. It is God's creation, after all, and after the waterfall experience, I now know what it means not just to live on the earth, but in communion *with* it.

Don and I discussed the property purchase decision at length.

"Don't you think this land would be something you would enjoy? You grew up in a rural setting; I think you would like it," I began.

"I am enjoying my retirement; I am happy with our Plano home and am not interested in taking that kind of risk or making that kind of investment," Don responded.

Umm... I thought, this is not going to be easy. "I need a place to relax more; a place to wind down; a place to feel connected to nature more," I persisted.

"You may need that, and I will not stand in your way; just don't expect me to spend a lot of time out there," Don concluded.

I tried again with the children. "I am excited about some land I have found in East Texas. It could be a great place for you and the grandchildren to come. What do you think?" I asked Wendi and Trey.

"We think it would be great for you, but don't expect us to come out much. Our lives are full on the weekends with the children's sports and other activities. Don't do this for us." In the end, I decided it was the best thing to do for my emotional and spiritual well-being. I did not want to live with regrets. So, after praying about it and discussing it with a few other people, I took the plunge. That summer I became a landowner at the age of 63 and purchased 20 acres in East Texas.

East Texas covers over 28,000 square miles, ranging from the Piney Woods bordering Louisiana and Arkansas to the prairies on the eastern edge of the Dallas-Fort Worth metro area, and from Oklahoma south to the lakes, wetlands, and beaches of the Gulf of Mexico.

Many who call this area home know it's a hidden gem resplendent with natural beauty and coniferous forests with many different species of pine trees. A number of hardwoods grow well in this region, including oak, hickory, and red maple. Many flowering trees are found in the area as well, including magnolias and wisterias.

The region is known for moderate rainfall, which keeps everything green year-round and makes it a great place to grow both flowers and vegetable gardens. Some parts here are wetter than others, making it an intriguing region ecologically where forests and wetlands exist, in some places, side by side. A great deal of wildlife calls East Texas home, including white-tailed deer, gray foxes, cottontail rabbits, and northern mockingbirds.

Buying 20 acres of East Texas land was a huge step for me and definitely outside my comfort zone. Since I had become a wife and a mother at a fairly young age and spent much of my professional life as an associate pastor, I had not made many major life decisions alone. There was usually someone around to consult, but I knew that this was one of those decisions I had to make on my own. It was another part of growing up for me—moving toward being more self-defined. That was probably one of the reasons I was so drawn to it.

I felt as called to buy the property as I had been called to go to seminary. My soul longed for growth, and while it was happening in my current home and work environment, I believed this new setting would invite deeper change inside of me. I also knew that buying land involved a lot of responsibilities, and while I certainly was not a farm girl, this girl who grew up in the country needed a slower pace and a calmer setting, a place that invited listening as much as doing.

I first tried to justify the purchase in business terms—the property would increase in value; the interest rate was low. It was a good investment. The more important factor, however, was not the business part, but that I liked the adventure of a new challenge. I longed for something that would stretch me, even propel me forward to the next part of my journey. The land delivered that in spades.

I first dealt with the business part of purchasing the property—so many details. The road had to be rebuilt, and the tenants in the mobile home I had purchased as a part of the property were having all kinds of problems and did not want to move. I didn't like dealing with conflict and tried to avoid it at first, but it soon became clear I had to be firm—not usually my long suit.

"Could you be gone by the first of next month?" I asked, hoping for the best.

"We are not sure. We must find a place to relocate."

After a few months of receiving no rent from them even though they were still there, I felt in over my head, and offered to help them move. Once they did make it out, I was so relieved. A friend came out and helped me clean and clean and clean. It took us three days, but it felt good that it was my property and my mobile home.

The seed had been planted on that beautiful, even magical, Hawaiian island where I stood under a remote waterfall; I was now falling in love with the hills, trees, and charm of East Texas. What I once might have seen as plain and ordinary was instead beautiful and had all kinds of possibilities. I was a little overwhelmed with what I did not know, but my optimism kicked in, and I began to appreciate the strengths I did have—intuition, relationships, passion, curiosity.

Like all good things, the change did not come easily. The summer of 2011—the first summer I owned the land—was one of the hottest in recent history. A severe drought killed more than half the trees on the property. I thought I could balance that by planting 1,000 pine seedlings along one of the fences on my property, but almost all of them died, partly because of the clay soil and partly because they did not have enough water.

Since I was hoping to tune into the ways that God speaks, I began to feel that the land was speaking to me, and I knew I wanted to listen. The trees that had made it through seemed to be sturdy enough to outlast anything. They now stood out instead of blending in.

I realized that in hard times the strong survive and then thrive. I loved the fact that there were so many different types of trees on the property—pine, oak, spruce, pecan, mimosa, and in later years dogwood, Bradford pear, maple, redbud, magnolia, and even peach—reminding me of the need for diversity in almost all areas of my life.

The noise of the bulldozers arrived on the land to push down and clear away what was now broken and dead so that the new could emerge. I met men like Ray, who drove the bulldozer, and who said to me, when I was concerned about cost, "I'm gonna be fair with you." I believed him, but nothing prepared me for what I saw when I drove out the first day of the clearing. It was a raging inferno!

Four or five fires were blazing—all at the same time—in big fire pits. It seemed to me as if everything was out of control, and it could have been a movie about the end of time, but Ray and his son both appeared very calm. My fear soon turned to excitement. I wanted to see every part of this activity, and when Ray asked at the end of the day, "Did you get your money's worth?" I said with a sense of awe, "That and so much more."

When Ray ground the stumps and cleared the creek, we discovered springs flowing from the Neches River. What joy! We had not seen them before, and I decided to call the land, "Hidden Springs." I thanked God. They were hidden from me no more.

As the sun was setting in the distance, Ray said, "On some jobs I don't make anything; on others I do. That is not the most important thing because my son over there loves it like I do. When we get on a bulldozer, everything else fades away and nothing else matters." I had heard others talk about following their passion and how important it was to stay close to the land because of what it did for their soul. Like a pioneer woman claiming her land, I now understood what they meant.

The bulldozer appeared again to dig the lake, which was to become my favorite spot. I worried that it would just be a big mud hole, that it would leak, that it would be too small, but in the end the land spoke, and everything worked. It only took a few weeks, but somehow, the whole world changed. There was now water where there had once been land. The beauty, the magic, the peace—it was all right there on my land.

Birthing the Cottage

More than three years later, on February 14, 2014, I signed the contract to construct an 1,175 square foot cottage on the property, which turned out to be the perfect size. I did the background work, selected a builder, and talked to the bank about the loan—all new experiences for me. I turned to key women in my life to help with details, and Camille Toro, my real estate and decorator friend, proved invaluable. I was so excited that I could not sleep. I was more than happy. I was experiencing deep joy.

On February 25, the builder put down stakes for the house. With Camille's help, I made a key decision to move the cottage closer to the water, which turned out to be the perfect location. Again, the land had spoken, and just as important, I had listened. On March 14, I met with the electrician, and he ran electric lines underground. By April, I signed the papers to borrow the money and was off and running.

It was the view that I cared most about. I wanted to open up the cottage, not close it in, for I had learned that more than anything, I hated to be boxed in. On the first try I had the ceiling too low. It was raised much higher, and on that first morning when I woke up in the brand-new cottage and looked out the windows, my heart skipped a beat. There it was—the openness, the sense of beauty and wonder my soul had longed for.

Colors were also a big deal for me. I chose strong vibrant colors for the interior—colors that said *Yes*—yellow, turquoise, tangerine, red. I was enjoying my newfound confidence and loved making my own decisions.

Part of the dream for the land had been that my loved ones would spend time together there, and I was deeply grateful when every family member was able to come to the newly finished cottage in November 2014. That Thanksgiving we celebrated my mother's 92nd birthday. The grandchildren caught fish, and five-year-old Landry slept in the top bunk saying, "I want to stay for a week!" Steve, my brother-in-law, made a fire out by the pond, and we all told family stories, the kind we liked the most. We talked about growing up and playing basketball, about the grandchildren playing soccer and baseball, about hunting and fishing. We talked about going on picnics and summer family vacations, about favorite movies and musicals. My brother, David, kept saying, "This is so much better than I expected!" Even though David is eight years younger than me, I now feel closer to him than I ever have before. I love seeing him thrive in retirement after a successful career in accounting management with an energy company in Houston (he was always good with numbers and statistics), and I can see that sense of contentment in him that I saw in our father later in his life.

I cherished this family time because I knew that it was special. I knew we would probably not all be together in this setting again. The evening ended when Kamryn, one of the grandchildren, spotted a skunk, of all things, and everyone scattered. The most important memory, however, was sharing the experience with my mom. She had been showing the beginnings of dementia, but on this day, she was *with* us, sitting and enjoying the view on the back porch, fully present. She kept saying, "I love being here. The land is beautiful. I love being with my family." Thank you, God.

Mystical Moments

Today, the cottage is being used in many different ways, often as a retreat for family or friends. But it also remains my own special place. It is a place to sip tea while sitting on the back porch, to go barefooted, to see the stars and moon at night, to see the sunrise in the morning and the sunset in the evening, to hear the birds, listen to the chimes, marvel at the wind blowing across the pond, observe the deer running early in the morning, watch the windmill turn, listen to the waterfall, and just sit on the front porch and absorb the natural beauty. Here, I can hear His "still small voice" (1 Kings 19:12) when I listen.

In this kind of setting, it was easy to open my heart more. I turned to people who understood the beauty of nature and wrote about these types of moments. I read "mystic mentors" like author and theologian Howard Thurman. He talked to trees and plants, and his profound love of nature gave him peace when he was lonely. It was Thurman who first helped me see and embrace the mystic side of myself. He spoke of the power of focusing on one thing for an extended period of time—seeing the beauty and awe of a small flower or plant, being fully present in the moment, and feeling connected through that moment to all of creation. I thought of Drake, my six-year-old grandson, and his sense of wonder and awe and his intense love of that which is simple and yet beautiful. He is blessed with a beginner's mind, as some would call it. I wanted to join him in seeing life that way.

It was at the cottage that I first discovered that I did not have to understand and analyze everything—major progress for me as one who spends too much time in my head. It is freeing not to have to filter everything through my brain! I am rediscovering that spirituality is not so much about claiming certain beliefs as it is about loving the human journey and living it with all its wonder. I experience magic moments there—moments of delight when the sun goes down with a blaze of glory. Sometimes I feel as if I am experiencing my own light show with the full moon on one side and beautiful shades of azure, sapphire, and cobalt in the clouds on the other side.

The birds twitter above, the pond sparkles, ice cold lemonade slides down my throat, and a crisp, clean scent fills the air after a recent rain. The beauty of all of it comes together in such a wonderful way, and everything feels connected. At times it almost feels like too much—too much to behold, too extraordinary, too much to bear. My heart aches with love for it—all of it. Francis of Assisi was right: "In God's world, everything is sacred." I finally have the eyes to see it—to behold it.

My Mother, My Self
When I made important decisions about the cottage, I often thought of my mom.

I recently re-read Nancy Friday's 1977 bestseller book, *My Mother/My Self: The Daughter's Search for Identity*, in which she confesses that she had spent most of her life explaining how she was different from her mom in an effort to separate from her. To her dismay, at the end of the book, she discovers the qualities she is proudest of in herself she had learned from her mom. I realized I had done the same thing. It took me to the end of my mother's life before I could see that she was strong in the areas of life that are most important to me— being real, being humble, being faithful, being resilient.

My mother was so much more than a teacher; she was a mentor and leader for hundreds of girls who needed her; no student was left behind. At her funeral (she died in July of 2022), several students came up to my sister and to me, saying, "Your mom helped me have good self-esteem." "She taught me to sew and have a sense of style." "She helped me with my homelife." "She taught us to have good manners and to bake special dishes." "She was always available when I sought her advice." "She helped me stay in my marriage." "She believed in me and gave me hope." "She never gave up on me."

An amusing story my sister tells about Mom highlights her organizational skills. It was field day at the memory care unit where she lived, and it was time for everyone to get on the bus to make the trip to an outdoor garden. The aides were nowhere to be found—there was an emergency somewhere else. Mom took the lead and went from one room to the next, probably eight in all, encouraging the women and men to all come out to the hallway and get in line for the trip. She was very successful, and when the aides finally returned, they were amazed that almost every one of the 75 or so residents were in line, eagerly waiting to board the bus. They had all followed Mom's orders!

In *Women Who Run with the Wolves: Myths and Stories of the Wild Woman Archetype*, Dr. Clarissa Pinkola Estés writes, "The daughters of your daughters of your daughters are likely to remember you, and most importantly, follow in your tracks." I believe this! The females in our family are connected, and great women tend to raise great women who in turn raise great women.

I want to celebrate the fact that the relationship with my mother was the first, the most lasting, and the most crucial relationship in my life; it impacted my journey like no other. And the legacy she leaves is not just for me; her inner strength and resilience are needed by all her children, her four grandchildren, and her eleven great-grandchildren. This includes her son, her grandsons, and her great-grandsons.

I also celebrate the fact that my mother's mother, Edie McGaha Roberts, husband to Jesse and mother to nine, was strong, self-defined and educated to be a teacher in an era when this was rare. She was a "great woman who raised a great woman."

It's Just a Stage

When Wendi and Trey were toddlers, becoming independent, and saying "No!" a lot, I found great comfort in saying to other parents, "It is just a stage." I was implying that this attitude was temporary and that easier times were ahead. This stage would not last forever.

The idea of stages in our adult lives became popular in 1976 when Gail Sheehy wrote her best-selling book, *Passages*, in which she stated that there was a predictable pattern in our adult lives. Then Dr. James Fowler, a professor at Candler School of Theology at Emory University, introduced the concept of stages of faith development in 1981.

I know that people do not fit neatly into any kind of category—they are too complex—but it is good to know that since the faith journey is primarily a journey about what it means to be human, there are certain common characteristics found in the faith journeys of not just traditional faith communities but also in all religious bodies. I believe that these common characteristics can tie us all together and help us to understand and appreciate differences.

When American psychiatrist and best-selling author M. Scott Peck took Fowler's six stages of faith and condensed them to four stages of spiritual development, he named them lawlessness, letter of the law, inquisitiveness, and spirit of the law. Peck also made it clear that the spiritual journey is unending for those who are curious enough to pursue it.

Many women are now naming the steps or stages in their own faith journeys; two I particularly appreciate are Barbara Brown Taylor, an Episcopal priest, and Elizabeth Elliot, a missionary to Ecuador. Taylor uses the language of Finding, Losing, and Keeping to describe the movement in her journey, while Elliot frames her faith journey as moving through Beginning and Becoming before she discovers Being. These verbs reinforce what other theologians write about as the life journey of any institution or church—building up, struggling, then integrating with more strength and clarity of mission.

There is the paradox again; another truth that is counterintuitive. After going up, you and I (and institutions) have to go down by surrendering to what cannot be controlled, and then face, rather than deny or avoid, the tragic, the sorrowful, the painful, even the unjust—all these things that can take us to the very bottom. Only then can people (and churches) genuinely put the first parts of the journey together and move forward toward true transformation.

Rohr observes that "God uses the very thing that would normally destroy people to transform them." I think he is right. Instead of feeling sorry for ourselves and being victims when things are difficult, we can discover that we are not alone, that God is present with us through all of it. We can be "saved" by God's grace.

A New "Method"
The Methodist movement's history traces back to 18th-century England, when preacher John Wesley proposed a "method" for encouraging deeper commitment to the Christian life; it involved small group meetings and an emphasis on holiness and service. In the United States, this movement grew quickly in the 19th century as circuit riders crisscrossed the country preaching and establishing churches. Partly because women were included in these small groups, sometimes as leaders, Methodists have ordained women since the 1950s, a topic that has divided many Protestant traditions but remains uncontroversial within Methodism.

Maybe Wesley was ahead of his time (although he had a lot of company) in calling the church to a both/and approach, long before that phrase was used, and long before many of us discovered that truth can be found in the tension between two ideas or two ways of thinking. I believe that a more nuanced way of thinking—being comfortable with subtlety and complexity—is needed in the 21st century as churches move through the first stage (going up) of their development and the second stage (falling down) toward an integration and depth that only comes through struggle and becoming humbler and more dependent on God. Either/or thinking which so often leads to division must take a backseat to both/and thinking where common ground is found.

And, instead of reaching only people like ourselves who have the same kind of beliefs and the same kind of backgrounds, we want to follow in the footsteps of those first Methodist women who were on the forefront of the 18th century revival in the Church of England. It is no accident that they tended to reach those who were often left out by the established church—the working class, the common people, those on the fringes of society. These are the very people we want to reach today!

These early days of Methodism also teach us the importance of empowering the laity and building bridges to groups outside the institutional church; since every Christian is called to serve, clergy like me need to get out of the way and let God work through lay leaders to invite, to greet, to teach, to serve, and to give. Small groups and classes lead the way.

As I look back at my more than 40-year ministry, I realize it was the laity who were there again and again doing what was needed. I came to see them as partners with me who were equally devoted to the task before us. I think of women like Priscilla Rau, who faithfully stood by me and helped as we started one new class after another at Custer Road UMC. I think of Frank Jackson and Dan Garner, who patiently served as peacemakers during a time of conflict at Lovers Lane. I think of so many others who helped me, even rescued me, when I was in over my head with some project or initiative.

And today, it is the women and men in my spiritual growth class that I teach each Sunday who are impacting me the most and helping me grow in my faith. I am not so much teaching them as I am walking alongside them, delighting with them in what we are all learning together as we fall in love more deeply with Jesus. It is truly a "revolutionary process," as one of the women said recently—one in which they pastor me as much as I pastor them.

Forever Young

I am so grateful that I have a place like the cottage in East Texas that reminds me of the wonderful truth that I can keep growing and learning for the rest of my life. There is so much still to learn. I am not a grown-up yet! I once thought if I could just focus on growth, I would eventually get there; I would become a mature adult. But now I see that the growth curve just keeps expanding and getting wider and broader and deeper. The process never ends.

This is very exciting; you and I can be forever young. The key is to stay humble, be curious, and be receptive. Just as I discovered underneath the waterfall on that Hawaiian island in 2010, God is continually and constantly inviting me to so much more than I am currently experiencing.

I saw this kind of attitude in a few of my teachers, friends, and colleagues when I was a young adult; they were what I considered old in years but were not at all set in their ways. Instead, they approached life with an open mind and were constantly engaged in learning new things.

I also noticed this kind of curiosity in a few of the women in our church who lived to be 100 years old or more. Babs Owen was one of those. She continued to read, to play cards, to have good conversations, to give to others, and to be active up until her death at 104. She made a difference in every group she was a part of and loved to help start new ministries in the church and in the community. She remained a good conversationalist her entire life and was always ready for the next challenge. I want to be like her.

I also want to be comfortable around people who have different opinions than I do. I want to be open enough to learn from them. One of the women in the class I am teaching spoke up recently, "I don't like this book we are reading. It all sounds too simple—almost like magic. I don't relate to that and am surprised you chose it."

Trying not to be defensive, I replied, "It is strong stuff—very definite and does not leave much wiggling room."

"Yes," she responded, "The author seems to be so certain he is right about everything. I have a book I want to suggest next."

"Sounds good; I will look at it," I concluded.

She and others are teaching me that those of us in the church can come across as judgmental and arrogant, even hypocritical, thinking that we have it all figured out. Clergy often like to be seen as experts who have nothing more to learn. This is a problem! Where did our humility go?

In a personality test a few years ago, I had an extremely high score on resisting structure. My colleagues commented on my score, asking, "What is that all about?"

I smiled and said, "I hate feeling boxed in. I don't even like getting into elevators!" It is true; in almost every area of my life, I want to soar, not be confined.

If I want to be forever young, then I will embrace other ways of seeing the world other than mine. I will get out of my box and my way of looking at the world long enough to appreciate those who have a different, perhaps larger view and a wider perspective.

In this seventh decade of life, my new vision is leading me to deeply explore topics with a hard-won wisdom, truth, and

Stepping Out

at times, unflinching vulnerability—emerging as the woman I only dreamed of becoming as a small-town basketball-playing church-loving country girl from Kilbourne, LA.

Chapter Eleven

Working On It

I did then what I knew how to do. Now that I know better, I do better.

—*Maya Angelou*

Parkland Moves Us

The spring of 2018 was filled with tension, and Lovers Lane UMC was no exception. The tragedy of the mass shooting at Marjory Stoneman Douglas High School in Parkland, Florida, had occurred in February. The incident was the deadliest mass shooting at a high school in U.S. history. Students from around the U.S. had organized the biggest ever "March for Our Lives" in Washington D.C. As a result, several church members pulled together and organized an event for Palm Sunday called "Parkland Moves Us." Lovers Lane UMC invited Justin Irwin, one of the teens who had been at school the day of the shooting and lost his best friend in the gunfire.

I Am Enough

He was a polite teenager and a good athlete with a deep faith and plans for a military career. He was not the kind of student who yearned for the limelight, but his life had changed profoundly that day when 17 of his classmates were killed. By no coincidence, he was a member of a United Methodist church, and this church was connected to Lovers Lane UMC through one of our members.

That Palm Sunday night at Lovers Lane UMC, Irwin bravely told us what happened. February 14, 2018, started like any other day, but the school soon went into lockdown when a fellow student started firing. Like many of his peers that day, he frantically sought safe shelter and texted his closest friends. Nineteen-year-old Nikolas Cruz had opened fire on students and staff, killing 17 people and injuring 17 others. Cruz, a former student at the school, fled the scene on foot by blending in with other students and was arrested without incident approximately one hour and 20 minutes later in nearby Coral Springs.

"The anxiety of not knowing if the people I cared about were safe was unbearable," Irwin explained. When Irwin's friend, Nick Dworet—co-captain of the swim team with him—did not respond, he continued to call again and again and hold out hope, but the next morning he learned the truth. "Nick meant a lot to me," he said in a trembling voice. That was all that needed to be said.

When he finished speaking, a standing ovation full of emotion erupted, which Jacquelynn Floyd—a writer for the *Dallas Morning News*—called a group hug. She concluded, "It was activism in a lower key than the marches, but it was activism just the same."

Stan commented, "Everybody needs to be heard."

After Irwin's speech, we divided into small groups to discuss this hot button topic. People were at different places on the issues but respected each other and engaged in civil dialogue. No one expressed rage, yelled, or put others down. Thanks to Irwin's steady lead, people were able to discuss their thoughts in a way that eased—instead of heightened—divisions. I was very moved that night. Justin found his voice as he expressed his grief openly, and everyone listened. Each of the invited politicians took turns giving possible solutions for gun violence. In that pivotal moment for our country, Lovers Lane UMC was able to be a voice for all who were ready to be heard.

"Parkland Moves Us" was one of the most important events ever held at Lovers Lane UMC. There were all kinds of people there, both from within the church community and outside it. It felt like the church had modeled something different than the standard debate. Instead, it had offered the hope of working together to address the country's biggest issues, while remembering that what holds people together is so much bigger than that which divides them. The United

Methodist connection worked, but more importantly, civility and reverence for humanity won. People were treated with respect—even when they held different opinions.

Unfortunately, even as I write, there have been several recent tragedies related to gun violence in schools. They appear to have escalated. I know there are no easy solutions, but I do know that churches must continue to have uncomfortable conversations about uncomfortable topics and put listening to each other front and center. Just as Justin did not have to say much on the night he spoke, maybe our attentive presence is more important than knowing what the exact solution is. It starts with coming together and listening to each other.

Out of Control

On Sunday, April 22, 2018, I had one of those meaningful moments—a moment that seemed to symbolize a new kind of honesty and authenticity, along with a new ability to be vulnerable and open to deeper feelings. I was helping to lead worship—as I had done in one way or another for nearly 40 years—when I was overcome with gratitude for the significant events and changes that I had experienced at Lovers Lane UMC for the last two decades.

The Holy Spirit was present that day, and worship seemed to gain momentum and energy with each part of the service—the opening prayer by a child, special needs women and men helping with ushering, the sign-language choir singing, Stan's convicting sermon, and the beauty of the words of the hymn "Savior Like a Shepherd Lead Us." By the time I got up to lead the offertory prayer, I was so filled with deep joy that tears began to flow.

Lovers Lane had been a stretching place for me, providing so many experiences that I would not have been comfortable with prior to my arrival. There had been ups and downs along the way, but that day I could see just how much the church had changed me in my inner being—in my soul. All kinds of people—people who are usually left out—were included, and I was deeply moved by that.

I thought I could handle my emotions. After all, I had told many parishioners—especially if they had experienced a loss—that it was healthy and healing to cry because it means that God is near, and they are feeling His presence. I had even said if they don't cry, chances were good they were dead emotionally. But here I was—a leader in worship—not wanting to call attention to myself, not wanting to be a distraction, not wanting to be this vulnerable.

I wasn't just shedding a few tears; I was weeping—openly, in front of the entire congregation. My emotions were on full display, and I could not stop them. Panic rose as I continued to cry not only during my part of the liturgy but during the congregation's part too! I struggled through the words. I felt exposed, embarrassed, and uncomfortable as I finished the prayer and stumbled back to my seat. The congregation—ever gracious—acted as if nothing unusual had happened. But I was in distress.

In my head I knew it was healthy for me to model vulnerability to the congregation; joy and gratitude were good signs of vibrant worship. I had certainly seen other ministers cry at the pulpit. But for me, this kind of display felt awkward, over the top, like I had made some kind of terrible social mistake. I did not want to be this REAL in such a public way. The lack of control rattled me.

It took a while for me to let my heart and soul hear that maybe I needed to experience being out of control more often. Was it possible I had become overwhelmed with feelings of gratitude for some really meaningful times in the church? And if so, maybe it was a good thing instead of a bad thing. Would people think less of me if I removed my armor? And did their judgment matter anyway?

I had been programmed to believe that being out of control is bad—socially unacceptable, showing a lack of restraint. But something broke through that Sunday morning in April that I could not control and that was important. In her book, *Daring Greatly: How the Courage to Be Vulnerable Transforms the Way We Live, Love, Parent, and Lead*, Brené Brown writes about "emotional exposure" being a good thing. I did not like feeling unsettled, even anxious, but once I got past my embarrassment, it felt good to be real and authentic. If vulnerability helps me be transformed in living, loving, parenting, and leading, then I am all for it. Maybe it was good that I had finally allowed God's presence to break through.

In fact, I am praying for more of those kinds of moments.

Don's Stroke
Many of my friends, as they grow older, have had a health crisis of some sort in which they had to pause, pay attention, and adjust their lifestyle. Mine happened when I was 64. Don's wake-up call came eight years later, on September 5, 2018, when he suffered a stroke. He had always exercised and was an avid runner, so we thought he was protected from something serious. We did not think a health crisis like a stroke could happen to him. We were wrong.

He alternated in the first few days after the stroke between being depressed or confused. I went from feeling really, really scared to believing that "everything would be just fine." It was a strange and unsettling time—changed our lives forever—and I wanted to be there for him. Trey and Wendi provided solid support and helped in many ways.

After his stroke, Don stayed in the hospital for physical therapy, so we were very relieved when he was finally discharged, hoping that things would soon return to normal. I kept having dreams about losing things, probably pointing to the fact that he and I were both losing our old way of life as we moved forward to a new, unsettled future—in uncharted waters. We both tended to be independent, feeling that we were somehow still in charge, which was not the case.

We slowly lived into a new kind of vulnerability. Neighbors and friends brought us food and volunteered to drive Don to physical therapy. Trey and Wendi gave us more attention and helped us make some decisions. For the very first time in his life, Don said, "I don't know what to do."

The biggest adjustment, however, was the new emotional side of Don. Before his stroke, he'd seldom shown emotion; he just was not wired to do that. Now he cried easily when anything emotional about himself or our family came up— partly because of the way the stroke had affected him—and a whole new side of him was uncovered. He was uncomfortable with this vulnerability and kept saying, "I wish I could stop crying." I kept thinking he was catching up for all those years he was unable to show much emotion or cry.

On Don's 77th birthday, two weeks after the stroke, we celebrated. It was not the usual kind of birthday celebration. So much had changed. That night we were deeply grateful that he was home—*home!*—and that he was alive, well, and could walk all through the house. Nothing else mattered much. One step at a time, we would move forward together. And we did.

Today, I continue to appreciate the new, vulnerable, more dependent side of Don. I have watched him struggle as he returned for the most part to his old self physically, while being a new person on the inside. He is more family-oriented, talks often on the phone with our children and grandchildren. They love to talk to him, and Wendi calls almost daily.

Our love has grown; we encourage each other, communicate more often, and don't take each other for granted as much. I see his tender side more often. Things that were once important don't seem to be all that important any longer. We certainly no longer see ourselves as invincible. We know what it means to be afraid and to live in fear. We have experienced what it is like to be in pain—both physical and emotional—and to come out on the other side.

No wonder that Richard Rohr states in his book *Falling Upward* that people have to fall down—to struggle, to suffer in some way, to make mistakes—before they are ready to embrace a deeper and more fulfilling life. I believe that. Don and I struggled, fell, and were humbled, leaving more space for the Holy Spirit to guide us. We lost some of our naivety and innocence as we moved toward becoming more human and fully present to the moment, realizing that each moment is precious and, sometimes, full of surprises.

A God of Surprises

Early in my ministry I heard a sermon about God being a God who surprises us, and it stayed with me, especially when I began to experience that aspect of God. Have you noticed? God does not usually do things the way people expect or plan for. He always has a much better way, something people could never dream up on their own. I need to be reminded of this surprise element regularly since I love to plan. Hmm… I can see God smiling now.

In January 2019, Lovers Lane UMC kicked off a capital campaign involving over and above giving for campus items and debt retirement. A series of dinners for donors set the tone for getting leadership on board. I thought I knew how to lead these campaigns. I was confident; I was in my comfort zone, and I was certain I knew what to expect.

Before these dinners, both Stan and I made one-on-one calls to several donors. To my surprise, some of the major donors from our traditional service, on whom we had relied in previous fundraising ventures, were unable to contribute. I had no idea what to do. Maybe the capital campaign would have to be put on hold, I thought.

Then, one of the calls I made was to a gay couple, Bruce and Dave, who were active and committed to our modern worship service called Crosswalk. When I invited them to one of the leadership team dinners, I also asked Bruce to share his personal story with the group. He agreed to do that.

Bruce began, "I am excited about this campaign and what it can mean for our church. Dave and I are going to give to it because we want to give a message of support to Lovers Lane, a church that embraces all kinds of people." He continued, "That has not always been our experience in other churches, but it is our experience here. We want anyone out in the community who is looking for a church home to know that they will be welcomed here." Then he added, "I am also part of an AA group that has been life-changing for me. We will support that ministry here also."

I found Bruce's testimony riveting. He was being so honest, so real, and I could tell this was natural for him because he often spoke like this. I was reminded how powerful this kind of sharing in a public setting can be. He was modeling not only generosity to the group but also being authentic and open. Later, Stan and I discovered that Bruce and Dave's commitment was the largest gift Lovers Lane UMC was to receive in the capital campaign.

Let's see now—the largest gift was not from the traditional service where the church had received them in the past. Instead, it came from an unexpected place—the smaller Crosswalk service. The gift was not a standard gift, as important as those are. It was an over-the-top, very generous gift. The gift was not just for the campus facilities that had been highlighted in the campaign; it was also for a ministry that was changing thousands of lives by emphasizing being honest and real. And it certainly hadn't come from our typical donor demographic, but from a gay couple.

Why was I so surprised? God seems to want to toss aside our way of thinking again and again and come up with something much better—something unpredictable and unexpected—something unplanned. I suppose it is one way God gets our attention, since we tend to limit ourselves to our own ideas instead of truly listening to God. And when God finds people like Bruce and Dave who don't limit him or put Him in a box, He shows up. They knew how to listen.

And God spoke. I smile every time I see the two of them as I am reminded of their faithfulness and of God enjoying surprising us.

Revival

In the fall of 2019, after a contentious General Conference in 2018, The United Methodist Church was divided about where it was going in the future. As Lovers Lane UMC held home gatherings, someone from our Zimbabwean Fellowship suggested that the church host a revival. Stan liked the idea and asked DeDe Jones, one of the pastors, to lead the way.

The revival was to take place over three days and two nights, featuring three of our African-American colleagues as preachers. I was so glad Lovers Lane UMC was hearing from them. Like many of our big events, I could feel the excitement building as the first night approached. The greeters and ushers came early, and as the music began, it set the tone for us to genuinely praise God for the opportunity to worship together.

The choir from St. Luke Community Church in Dallas was inspiring. When they processed in, they did not just bring themselves; they brought the Spirit! Energy filled the room, and by the time Rev. Mike Bowie stood to preach, the congregation was more than ready to receive the Word. He challenged and inspired everyone not to just *do* church but to be the church. One thing was for sure—all would be the church together!

Why was worship so good that night? I wondered. I believed it was partly because people were worshiping with a community they loved and with whom they had a strong history. Everyone shared a common love for the people of Dallas and for The United Methodist Church. Each church had a history of being involved in the community and supporting city leaders who were working to change Dallas for the better. There was a strong bond, and we were not just worshipers—we were good friends who loved God, and we truly had something to praise God about. People stayed late at the reception afterwards, and no one seemed to want the magical evening to end.

Then on Sunday morning Dr. Zan Holmes preached. He was much loved by the Lovers Lane UMC congregation.

Today, Zan Wesley Holmes, Jr. is Pastor Emeritus of the large and influential St. Luke Community UMC in Dallas, Texas, where he served for 28 years. He was Adjunct Professor of Preaching at Perkins School of Theology at Southern Methodist University for 24 years. Known as much for his community activism as his preaching and teaching, Dr. Holmes was elected to the Texas House of Representatives from 1968 to 1972, while he also served as United Methodist District Superintendent.

In 1991, Governor Ann Richards appointed him to be the first African American to serve on the Board of Regents of the University of Texas System, a position he held from 1991 to 1997. In 1971, Judge William Taylor of the United States Court for the Northern District of Texas appointed him to serve as chairperson of the Tri-Ethnic Committee, which oversaw the implementation of public school desegregation in the Dallas Independent School District. In 2001, the National Voting Rights Museum and Institute in Selma, Alabama, recognized him as one of the civil rights movement's "Invisible Giants." He is widely respected by everyone who knows him and is known for his great preaching, as well as his leadership in the city.

Pastor Holmes brought the house down with his sermon about living into our uniqueness as individuals, saying, "Everyone else is taken!" He challenged people to live into who God has called them to be. Lovers Lane honored him that day, and he honored Lovers Lane.

After those three days in August, every good thing happening around the church seemed to be a little bit better. Every worship service seemed to be a bit more spirited; every potential new member seemed to be more eager to join. Every hymn was easier to sing, and every sermon was a little bolder.

We had been revived.

Going After the One
In my early years of ministry, I was trained that numbers mattered most in the church—number of first-time visitors on any Sunday, number of second-time visitors, number of phone calls made each week, and number of people who join. Keep the system moving and keep it efficient. Don't spend too much time on any one phone call or any one person. Contact and connect with as many people as possible. Save those souls, but even more, grow the church!

Like other times in my ministry, I discovered at Lovers Lane UMC that the old way was not necessarily the best way. In fact, my old way of thinking often hindered the new way, which was to listen to the Holy Spirit and let the Spirit lead instead of being driven by my need to boost my ego.

Bill Hutton taught me this truth.

Witnessing Bill Hutton and his wife Sue become members of LLUMC was one of the most wonderful adventures with God I have experienced. Bill was a doctor in his 70s who had lived a good life but was ready for more meaning. His wife Sue let him set the pace regarding church, and she came with him.

They visited Lovers Lane for the first time in 2017 and were struck by the richness of the music and the excellence of the preaching. They visited the church for more than a year before leaving any contact information, but at one point, Bill left their names on the visitor registration cards. I saw their names often, but I had never met them. One day before worship quite "by accident," I greeted a couple in the hallway and introduced myself to them. When he told me their names, my eyes lit up. Finally, I had discovered the mystery couple. He laughed about that and seemed to enjoy the interaction.

After that, he started leaving his phone number on the visitor card, and when I called him, he always answered his phone. He was not shy about telling me that he was an atheist, and I affirmed his questions and his atheism, wanting him to know that each of our journeys were different, and that almost all of us have doubts at times. I shared with him that one of my favorite theologians, Frederick Buechner, said, "Doubt is the ants in the pants of believing."

My discussions with Bill continued over a period of time, and one day I invited Sue and him to a lunch for visitors at the church. They were not able to attend but did encourage me to come by their home for a personal visit. A few days later I went to their home. There, I discovered that she was a talented artist who had a home studio where she pursued her passion. I loved seeing her creative space, along with his library which was stacked with books. I also got to meet their son who was an integral part of their lives. We talked about worship, the church, Stan's sermons, and their journey.

Within a month I asked Bill if he and his wife would like to talk about joining the church. I was a little surprised (O, ye of little faith) when he said that he was ready. In the next few weeks, the two of them became official members. The day they joined, Sue laughed, and said, "I still can't believe that you got Bill to join a church!"

And then I laughed, knowing it was not me but the Spirit moving in him, opening his heart, taking away his restlessness and doubts as they ever so gradually turned into the kind of faith and trust he had hungered for and sought but could not yet name. Since taking the step into church membership, Bill and Sue have become part of a class that fits them; they attend worship and serve regularly. They smile every time I see them. Bill has a gleam in his eye, and I think we both know we have gone through something important together.

I Am Enough

We are bound together in Christ, brothers and sisters in Christ. One who was lost has been found. One who was searching has found peace. One who was on the outside of the faith community has become an insider. And I, once again, have been humbled by this wonderful God who keeps showing me that while numbers can be a sign of a healthy organization, the wonder and awe that Bill and I share beats any spreadsheet anywhere. We love each other, and that is what real church and real life are all about.

I see now that this experience was preparing me for the next step—widening the circle and extending that kind of love to everyone and everybody.

Chapter Twelve

Welcoming Everyone

What makes the gospel offensive isn't who it keeps out, but who it lets in.

—*Rachel Held Evans*

Building Bridges

Because of Lovers Lane UMC's history, location, and the age of its members, funeral services for several celebrities have occurred at our church—Jerry Haynes (Dallas children's TV personality Mr. Peppermint), baseball player Mickey Mantle, Dallas Cowboys coach Tom Landry, and general manager Tex Schramm, to name a few.

Memorial services for the regular faithful members of Lovers Lane, however, are the ones I remember most. One of those special occasions occurred during Advent in 2019.

Ursula and Hall Harris came to Lovers Lane UMC a few years earlier because their son Mark was gay, and when the U.S. Supreme Court decision to legalize same-sex marriages was handed down on June 26, 2015, they decided it was time to move away from their Bible church and reclaim their Methodist roots. At that time, Hall was a New Testament professor at Dallas Theological Seminary, which is a well-respected, nondenominational graduate school.

It was the beginning of a great partnership between the Harrises and our church. Hall and Ursula served the church in many ways, including teaching a Sunday School class, and Lovers Lane provided a welcoming environment for all, including their son and others like him. Their faithful example as unconditionally loving parents had a positive impact on all of us.

This accepting atmosphere for gay couples and singles at Lovers Lane had not come about easily. Although Lovers Lane had long been known for being a welcoming community, it had been up to Stan to lead the church—long before most other churches did so—to a place of genuine acceptance.

Stan preached and taught, calling the congregation to a radical kind of love that made room for different ways of living this love out. He preached about sexuality and other social issues at times, making it clear that it was important to look at the deeper principles of scripture and see how God spoke through them. Because of his openness on the issue, Stan was able to bridge the divides in our community by making room for the full spectrum of opinions rather than telling congregants they had to take sides regarding the issue. He did not speak in absolutes and brought the church together by reminding people that they are all sinners in need of love and grace.

In 2014 a turning point occurred when a group of gay men asked Stan if they could meet as a small group in our church. Stan said yes, and the presence of Refuge, as the group was called, began to make a difference on our campus. A tense moment came during a Mother's Day worship service when a woman pastor with two gay sons surprised us all by calling for the gay people in the congregation to stand, causing a few people to leave the sanctuary. Then LLUMC had another first—our annual Everybody's Christmas event was led by a gay person, encouraging even greater diversity throughout the church. People in the African Fellowship in the church stated that although they might not all view homosexuality the same way Stan did, they believed in the church's vision of "Loving All"—keeping the church united.

None of us were prepared in early December 2019, when Ursula died peacefully in her sleep. She had health issues, but she was only 66 years old. She had given her testimony a few weeks before her death to the staff, and everyone who heard her was aware of her rich personal and professional life that was filled with goodness. We had all enjoyed learning about the Methodist roots in her German background and the way she had overcome many challenges, including limited eyesight.

It was in this context that Ursula's memorial service was held in the Lovers Lane UMC sanctuary. It was a beautiful service. Her son gave a great eulogy; her daughter sang "Be Thou My Vison" and "It is Well with My Soul," and Hall read a wonderful love poem he had written for Ursula. There were people there from Lovers Lane UMC who had been in worship and small groups with her, friends and neighbors from several other churches, and colleagues from Dallas Theological Seminary. All came to celebrate her life.

They stayed for what the bulletin called a "Kaffee and Kuchen reception," a German ritual where friends and family meet to enjoy coffee and cake and to socialize. It hit me as I looked around how happy it would have made Ursula that through the celebration of her life, she was bringing together people with different theological beliefs—people who had different ways of thinking about social issues and free will—but who were united in their love for Jesus, for her, and for one another. No one wanted to leave because there was so much good energy in the room. It was filled with love.

Conversations were going on; bridges were being built across the room, and the universal church that Ursula believed in so fervently was taking a step forward in embracing and loving each other, being the church at its best. Attendees at the service had found their common ground.

I did not want to leave. Ursula's life was so filled with all that is good and right, and I wanted that to linger. She had helped all of us take a step closer to the Kingdom and to the Church triumphant where God fully reigns. I thanked God for her life and for allowing her to come among us and show us the unconditional love that God has for each of us and for all of us.

Evolving Over Time

My own journey in relation to the lesbian, gay, bisexual, transgender, queer, intersex, asexual, or LGBTQIA+ issue, has evolved over time. I assumed when I went to seminary in 1977 that I would be able to discern the truth and rest more comfortably with my discoveries. After all, I had a lot of time and money invested in these classes with some very smart people, so the least I could expect was to find clear answers to all my questions. Right? Of course, it didn't really happen that way; I never got those right answers. Instead, I discovered many new questions.

I had pretty much avoided the "gay and lesbian issue" until the late 1970s, when the topic came up in a few of my theological classes and conversations with other students. At that point, I did not know anyone who was openly gay. By no accident, Dr. Ruth Tiffany Barnhouse was one of my first professors at Perkins School of Theology. She was not only a professor; she was the only female Episcopal priest in Dallas. She was also a psychiatrist who had studied both the world of medicine and the world of religion. Best known for being the psychiatrist of Sylvia Plath, she corresponded with her after they met at McLean Hospital in Belmont, Massachusetts, following Plath's breakdown in 1953.

I highly respected Dr. Barnhouse, and I listened to everything she said about women's identity, family and psychology, and interpretation of scripture.

It was her perspective on sexuality, however, that stayed with me the most. I remember our class discussion. "When it comes to living out our sexuality, I find it helpful to see people on a continuum—with one end representing the way we are created and the other end representing the environment in which we find ourselves," she began. "I understand people to be at different places on the continuum, and they can move along it. They don't necessarily stay in one place all their lives," she continued.

A continuum. There is that word again. So much for keeping things simple. Where were my answers? I did not want to have to struggle with this. I was merely trying to decide if gay and lesbian people should be accepted in the church. Yes or no. Should people try to change them? These were not Dr. Barnhouse's questions. Instead, she seemed to be able to see sexuality from different points of view and to stay neutral. She was very calm about the subject while most others I listened to were all whipped up about it. But, to my dismay, she wasn't going to give me a quick or easy answer to my questions. Instead, she challenged me and others to think—and to listen to the Holy Spirit.

I now realize that in every conversation I have had about sexuality in the last 40-plus years—and I am still having them—I think of what she taught. When people with whom I am discussing this issue seem to be certain they have it all figured out and use scripture to prove their positions, a warning light goes off in my head. I *always* mention the continuum.

I also had read enough of John Wesley by this time to realize that he often took the middle-of-the-road approach on social issues. He was wary of coming down strongly one way or another. I knew that he did not believe that we should separate our faith from science, for he believed that the two could and should go together. The scientific experts and scholars I read on the issue of homosexuality seemed to present different views, not coming to a firm conclusion one way or the other. In other words, they spoke of many different variables—hormonal, environmental, genetic, socialization, birth order, etc.—instead of one main factor.

My own perspective continued to evolve over time. After moving into the local church in the early '80s and serving for several years, I came down on the side that believed the church was not ready for the ordination of gay and lesbian clergy. That was my solution. It was not good for the church, and that was the most important thing. Now I could check that issue off my list. This resolution allowed me to step away from the controversy and put my focus on the other important thing—bringing people to Christ. It sounded very reasonable, I thought.

The only problem was that some people had already come to Christ, and they were gay, and a few of them were in our church. To add to this, one of them was feeling the nudge to go into full-time ministry and to serve God just like I had. Again, my desire for simplicity and avoiding conflict was not working. I was frustrated and unsettled—a difficult position for many in The United Methodist Church at the time and, most certainly, for me.

Close to Home

A major breakthrough on this aspect of my journey came when I fully engaged—and embraced—a nephew who is gay and comfortable with who he is. He is, in fact, impossible not to love and accept.

Two years before Don's stroke, in the summer of 2016, my friend Barbara and I took a trip to California, driving down the Pacific coastline. The highlight of that trip was visiting Don's nephew, Dustin Lance Black, who lived in Los Angeles. Don's sister, Anne (Lance's mother), had contracted polio when she was two years old. As a result, she endured numerous surgeries and used braces or crutches her entire life.

I remember Anne telling Don and me early in her marriage, "The doctors are really discouraging; they say I can never marry or have children, but I will not accept that." I was so glad she thought that way! I admired her through the years as she defied the doctors by falling in love, marrying, and then giving birth to three sons. She actually thrived as a mom as well as in her career, while being paralyzed from the waist down. It became so clear to me that she would never be a victim in any way. She believed she could do what everyone else could do and was a genuine inspiration to all of us. Sadly, Anne died in 2014, but not before leaving her son the most precious gift a mother could give: unconditional love and acceptance.

Lance was her middle son. He was very close to her, acknowledging that he had been very shy as a child, and he loved to spend time with her as she read aloud to him. As he wrote in his memoir, *Mama's Boy: A Story from Our Americas*, "Neither of us were a particularly good fit for this world." In the book, he explained that reading was a good way for him to escape, and because of it, he fell in love with the art of storytelling. He became very good at it.

After leaving Texas and moving to California when his stepdad accepted a new job there, Lance not only began to accept the fact that he was gay, but also found a way to use his love of storytelling in the theater. He went on to become a filmmaker and screenwriter who wrote the Oscar-winning screenplay for the movie *Milk*.

Milk is a 2008 American biographical film based on the life of gay rights activist and politician Harvey Milk, who was the first openly gay man to be elected to public office in California, as a member of the San Francisco Board of Supervisors. Directed by Gus Van Sant, the film stars Sean Penn as Milk, Josh Brolin as Dan White (a city supervisor), and Victor Garber as San Francisco Mayor George Moscone.

The film was released to critical acclaim and grossed $54 million worldwide. It earned numerous accolades from film critics and guilds for Penn's and Brolin's performances, Van Sant's directing, and Black's screenplay. It received eight Oscar nominations at the 81st Academy Awards, including Best Picture, and went on to win two: Best Actor for Penn, his second Oscar, and Best Original Screenplay for Lance.

Anne called Don and me in 2009; she sounded excited. "Lance has been nominated for an Academy Award! I am going to the ceremony."

Don was calm, but I could not believe it. I was so impressed that there was someone in the family like Lance. He was not even 40 years old, but he had already risen to the top of his field and was known as a powerful activist for those on the margins of society. He did win the Academy Award that night, but in his words, "The best and most important part of my life is yet to come." He decided that he had unfinished personal business from his past, and it was time to deal with his roots.

Lance began by confronting wounds from his childhood faith in the Mormon church. He traveled to Salt Lake City—to the heart of the Latter-day Saints—where he met with some of the leaders in the Mormon Church. He admitted that this meeting was tense at first. But when it became clear that each of them was there to share stories and not try to change the other, they started to build trust. That meeting then led to Lance and his friends being invited back to the Mormon Tabernacle Christmas Spectacular, which he called the "Mormon Oscars"—a televised event, hosted by a celebrity, with hard-to-come-by tickets.

At that event, he had a one-on-one conversation with a soft-spoken Mormon brother.

"You mean you want to have a family?" the Mormon friend asked, surprised.

"Yes, I very much want to get married and have children—and I want them to be safe."

The Mormon friend responded, with tears in his eyes, "I see..." This appeared to be a different way of seeing things for his new friend.

I saw Lance for the first time as an adult when he came back to Texarkana, Texas, in 2012 for the funeral of Anne and

Don's sister, Josie, who had been the matriarch of the family. Lance had decided it was time for him to return home—to the extended Southern family that his mom had grown up with, most of them living in or around Texarkana. At that point, his mom was not strong enough physically to attend the funeral in Texarkana, so she asked her sons—Todd and Lance—to go in her place.

Lance said that he knew that he must do what his mom asked, even though he had done a good job in the years before of keeping his distance from all that reminded him of the place he had once called home. To say the least, he was not the same shy guy who'd avoided any kind of attention or limelight. The family all knew that he had been at the forefront of much-needed national reform concerning social issues, and I could see why he might worry about how he would be received back home in this very conservative Texas town that was not known for embracing change. Don and I attended the funeral that day, and we walked to the gravesite with Lance and his brother Todd. I remember how proud we were that both of them were there.

On May 6, 2017, with many members of their families present, Lance married Thomas Daley at Bovey Castle in Devon, England, and on June 27, 2018, their first son was born in southern California.

Eight months earlier, on October 17, 2017, our son Trey and his wife Kylie welcomed their first son into the world.

Welcoming Everyone

The two boys will grow up together as second cousins, making the whole family proud.

In the spring of 2019, I saw Lance again. He came to Dallas to speak at the Cathedral of Hope—a congregation of the United Church of Christ and the world's largest primarily LGBTQ congregation—about his new memoir, *Mama's Boy*. We were in a church community with many races, ethnic backgrounds, religious experiences, ages, sexual orientations, and gender identities. "This is not a book about politics. It is a story of family foundations, turmoil, tragedy, and love," Lance began.

"Where did you grow up?" he was asked.

"I grew up poor and gay in San Antonio, Texas, with a mom who was married three times, who was physically disabled and who was deeply religious in the Mormon faith."

"What was your relationship with her like?"

"We were deeply bonded—even though we were very different in many ways."

"What did she teach you?

"She taught me that every single person on this planet is different from everyone else in at least one remarkable way. She taught me that it is our differences that make this world magical, entertaining, innovative, and downright livable. She taught me that a little Southern girl from the poorest city in America who couldn't take a single step because of her polio could have it all. Her life gives me hope for our future as a country." (Dustin Lance Black, *Mama's Boy: A Story from Our Americas* [Vintage Books, a division of Penguin Random House LLC, 2019], 194)

Later that day I was able to say to Lance what his courage and writing gift had done for the family. He had brought the siblings back together again, brought a sense of pride and dignity to a family that had suffered through more than its fair share of struggles, and encouraged us to face—rather than avoid—pain.

In June 2021, Lance came to Lovers Lane UMC and told his story, a story of hope, emphasizing that love is always more powerful than hate. Many in Don's family came also. Lance genuinely sought out those who saw things differently from him. He brought with him a crew who filmed part of a documentary about his life and his relationship with his mom. He interviewed all of us—including Don—asking about Don's memories growing up. Everybody cried. The documentary "Mama's Boy" aired in 2022.

Lance has been a writer and producer for other TV shows, most recently "Under the Banner of Heaven" which is based on an investigative book by Jon Krakauer. It tells of the chilling 1984 murder of a young woman and her daughter at the hands of her Mormon fundamentalist brothers-in-law. At the very least, the series shines light on the view that women should "stay in their place" and not question authority or their faith. Lance's mom would be so proud. I know that I am. On April 5, 2023, Lance Black and Tom Daley announced the birth of their second son, born on March 28, 2023.

Crosswalk
At Lovers Lane UMC, I developed good relationships with several men and women who are gay and worshiping in our modern service called Crosswalk. I discovered an interesting thing—they were struggling, too, with many of the same theological issues I wrestled with. It was good that we could talk about it and struggle together. We had found our common ground. One day, I found myself saying to a few members of the Crosswalk class, "Don't ever think you are not worthy in some way. You are as worthy as I am or any of my colleagues. None of us is perfect. You don't have to be either. You just need to be aware that you need God's grace like all of us do."

It was then I realized that I might not have an "answer" to my deeply rooted questions about homosexuality and God, but I did seem to have new spiritual wisdom. I had moved from tolerance to acceptance. Everyone is on the same journey of learning what it means to be human—broken people in need of grace. I am loved as I am, a heterosexual, and others who are of a different orientation are loved as they are, too.

It felt so freeing to fully embrace this truth, just like the night at "Everybody's Christmas" when I had fully embraced

Cadillac, my new homeless friend whom I knew had been sent to help me get over prejudice I had about homeless people. He helped me see that we are all alike.

These were both big steps for me—and important ones.

Then came the night in 2019 when the first openly gay woman in our conference, Jane Graner, was ordained. I cried, along with her and with many of my colleagues. It was a high and holy moment—much like the night I had been ordained, but this time it was not about me. It was about her and others like her. I could celebrate this holy evening with her because I believed she should be treated just like me—someone who believed she was called by God to serve Him although she was not perfect, just as none of us are. We are all on the journey of becoming fully human, seeking to know God more fully and acknowledging the need for God's grace as we move forward.

The Big Break

Not everyone was having the experiences that I was having in relation to LGBTQ issues. When The United Methodist Church decided to delay its General Conference (the decision-making body for the broader church) due to the pandemic and complications related to bringing the global church together, a more conservative group in the church decided the time was right to break away from The United Methodist Church and begin a new denomination which did not ordain or marry gay people. Some United Methodist churches, seemingly led by a desire for financial independence, used this time to join other denominations or to become independent. By the end of 2023, about a quarter of UMC churches had disaffiliated from the denomination, the majority of those being in the South.

Having experienced mergers and schisms in its history, today's United Methodist Church—by far the largest expression of Methodism—is moving forward with its worldwide approach and its mission to "Make disciples of Jesus Christ for the transformation of the world." As of 2020, before the Big Break, only the Southern Baptist Convention was bigger among Protestant denominations.

While United Methodists, like other mainline denominations in the US, have declined in numbers, the good news is that The United Methodist Church will more than likely continue to be the most culturally diverse mainline denomination in the world with a strong presence on four continents. This means The UMC will continue to serve the world-wide community of Christians in all its beauty and diversity!

What Is Our Future?

One thing I know for sure is that God's timing is always best, and it appears that several factors are lining up for The United Methodist Church to be ready to match the needs of an ever-changing world. Everywhere I look these days I see diversity growing, and diversity has always been a hallmark of our nation and of the United Methodist Church.

The 2020 Census shows that the overall US population is more racially and ethnically diverse than it was a decade earlier. By 2050, Hispanic residents are projected to account for a quarter of the US population, up from 19.1% today. African Americans are projected to make up 14.4% of the population in 2050, up from 13.6% currently. Asians will account for 8.6% of the population, up from 6.2% today. This is good news for our nation, and it is very good news for The United Methodist Church.

My own state of Texas, the second most populous state, is ahead of the diversity shift going on in our country. Texas' 2024 population of 31 million people has a majority of Hispanic residents, according to the U.S. Census Bureau. By 2036, when Texas will celebrate the start of its third century, the state is expected to have gained between three million and five million people. By 2060, an estimated 36 million to 44 million people will call Texas home.

What a great opportunity for United Methodists to expand our unique and balanced theology, share our brand of caring, and celebrate our connection with one another. This opportunity exists not only in Texas but throughout our country and the world. Building bridges and working across divides and cultural differences will be the order of the day, and our identity will continue to be shaped by John Wesley's comment, "If your heart is with my heart, then give me your hand."

Historically, it is important to remember that United Methodism has always been a denomination marked by both geographical and ideological diversity. Justice Harry A. Blackmun, who wrote the Supreme Court opinion establishing the right to abortion in *Roe v. Wade*, was a Methodist; so is President George W. Bush, who signed the Partial-Birth Abortion Ban Act 30 years later. At one time, both Laura and George W. Bush and Hillary and Bill Clinton attended the same United Methodist Church in Washington D.C. The list of 31 current members of Congress who are Methodist includes conservative Republican senator Tom Cotton of Arkansas and his progressive Democratic colleague Elizabeth Warren of Massachusetts.

It is also important to note that even though a number of conservative congregations have exited, The United Methodist Church of the future is still likely to be centrist—center right and center left—both theologically and socio-politically. This will likely be true not only in the US church but also in the world-wide United Methodist Church. This aspect of who we are is so important to recognize! United Methodism has never been and never will be a church that caters to the extremes. John Wesley's emphasis on "agreeing to disagree" will be very much a part of us in the future. That is one of the reasons that we offer—as a part of our mainline Protestant tradition—a variety of types of worship. We recognize that one size does not fit all. In other words, we honor and value diversity and differences. This is a big plus in the 21st century!

You can imagine my deep joy, then, when on May 3, 2024—at the United Methodist General Conference meeting in Charlotte, North Carolina—I watched as delegates representing Lovers Lane UMC, along with churches from all over the world, voted to remove the last barriers to full equality of LGBTQ+ members in the life of the church.

Just the day before, in another incredible moment, conference delegates repealed a hurtful and harmful 52-year-old declaration that the practice of homosexuality is "incompatible with Christian teaching." The passage in The UMC Book of Discipline, or church law, that states: "Ceremonies that celebrate homosexual unions shall not be conducted by our ministers and shall not be conducted in our churches," was eliminated.

Delegates also voted to remove provisions that would have charged clergy with immorality if they were not "faithful in a heterosexual marriage" or "celibate in singleness." Instead, delegates replaced that with a requirement of integrity in all personal relationships.

And, earlier that week at the Conference, delegates dropped a ban on the ordination of gay clergy. Most of the measures passed by a 3-1 margin.

The effect of all those measures was to expunge from the United Methodist Discipline rulebook all punitive measures against LGBTQ+ people, a striking change for the denomination, closing the chapter on more than 50 years of battles for mainline Protestants. To say the least, it is a new day and a new beginning!

I love the "About Us" wording on our denominational website that describes United Methodism as a worldwide connection of millions of members in Africa, Asia, Europe, and the United States. It says, "We are the person next door, the church on the other side of the country, and the worshiping community across the globe. Together, we share a legacy of living as disciples of Jesus Christ, sharing God's love both in what we say and how we serve our neighbors." May we live into this vision.

Bishop Mande Muyombo
This understanding of what is most important for the future of our denomination and for the church at large was clearly expressed by an African Bishop a few years earlier in January 2020 at Lovers Lane. Stan had invited him, along with a dozen other United Methodist clergy and lay leaders from Africa and the Philippines, to our church to further discern

wisdom for centrist Methodists who were seeking a way forward. This kind of gathering was possible because we are part of a connectional church that listens to one another—we do not stand alone and decide our future apart from our brothers and sisters around the globe.

Bishop Mande Muyombo is from the North Katanga province in the Democratic Republic of the Congo in Africa. He had been to Lovers Lane UMC once before with the Africa University choir. Muyombo was born in a poor family in Kambove village in Haut-Katanga province. His father had two wives and 16 children. Muyombo became an executive of the General Board of Global Ministries when he was elected on the fourth ballot during the Congo Central Conference in 2017. He was the first graduate of Africa University to be elected bishop and the youngest episcopal leader in the central conference.

Bishop Muyombo spoke clearly to my heart when he began, "The African church is over 100 years old; we are a mature church. We are familiar with scripture. We are very big on community, and it is not African to exclude other people."

Later he went into the role of both pastor and prophet as he stated in a very loving way that he wanted, on behalf of his people—whom he "held in his heart"—to acknowledge guilt and ask for forgiveness from all those who had been hurt by harsh words and rude behavior at the 2019 General

Conference of Methodism where LGBTQ issues exploded in acrimony.

He said that knowingly or unknowingly the church had demonized other people and that "he could not leave this place without acknowledging his guilt and saying, 'Forgive us. Let's work together. Let's focus on mission. Forgive us.'"

Out of all the wise and poignant things that were said that day, these words were the most powerful to me and were an invitation to change my attitude. I said a prayer that this could be the beginning of healing for all of us. I knew that all of us needed that. I knew that God was present, that He was moving among us, and I wanted to respond to what God was doing.

Bishop Muyombo spoke truth when he stated that the only way a church can be real and authentic and true to its calling is to learn to love and forgive. His words reinforced for me that it is not enough in the church to be successful and productive with lots of programs and outreach. That is a business approach, and our calling is so much more than that of a business. Real church involves being the Body of Christ by following Jesus and laying down our pride and egos, acknowledging our failures, asking for forgiveness, and beginning to really love one another. This depth in relationships moves us toward the true freedom that helps us serve God's purposes, not our own plans and purposes.

It hit me that day that churches are like people in that churches, too, must go through pain, struggle, even suffering before they become more compassionate, more caring, more empathetic, and more loving. They, too, have to mature and grow up and move out of their infancy when they were largely focused on themselves. Wonder of wonders—God moves and speaks as the Body of believers together discover humility and the need for God's grace. Bishop Muyombo was God's messenger to us that day. It was time to repent.

It is no surprise, then, that the authentic spiritual journey for a church—the one that leads to true transformation—is not easy. Repentance is hard! It is the opposite of what we normally do—charging ahead with our plans for church growth and new programs. It calls for stopping, listening, and being open to a change in our hearts. No wonder Jesus warned us when he said that not many would choose to go through the narrow gate, even though He makes it abundantly clear that He has much to offer those who do.

I knew I wanted to head toward that narrow gate—to be with people like Bishop Muyombo—to go on that kind of spiritual journey with him and with others. Thanks be to God—I was and am in a connectional church that brings someone from halfway around the world to encourage us to see the light.

Chapter Thirteen
Bringing Light

Nothing new happens without apology and forgiveness... The "unbound" ones are best prepared to unbind the rest of the world.
—*Richard Rohr*

The Further Journey
A few years ago, I was on a vacation with my family to the Rocky Mountains. I was comfortable taking a cable car up to what I thought was the top of the mountain. I am not particularly thrilled with heights, but I was with others, and we were inside a cable car. So, I was not anxious. We walked around once we got there and looked at the scenery. Then my brother made a suggestion, "We can go up even higher—to the top of the top of the top—by riding a ski lift that is open, not enclosed." I declined, saying, "I have seen all I want to see."

The two of us met a couple from Texas and began to chat with them. All of us were walking together along a path; I did not realize it, but all of a sudden, they took my hand. We all sat down at the same time—on the ski lift to the top of the top of the top. I wanted to get off, but it was too late. Much to my surprise and angst, I was riding up and up and up to the top, although I had definitely not planned to. When my new friends saw the look of fear on my face, they made sure they kept asking me questions to distract me and keep my mind off the ever-rising ski lift.

I was finally able to take a deep breath and look around; as we climbed; I caught a glimpse of things I had never seen before. It was beautiful—a different kind of beauty—not people, but trees and plants and birds and wildlife. It was very quiet and still—even serene, very peaceful. Those moments remain imbedded in my memory. I will never forget the experience.

I discovered a new world by going higher than I ever thought I wanted to. Other people I trusted helped me get there. And now that I was there, my view of the mountain had expanded and enlarged. I thought of this experience when I first heard Richard Rohr speak of the importance of what he calls "The further journey." Is this a way to describe the part of the faith journey that can only happen when people are being real, living real, and loving real—when people know they are complex, flawed, *and* beautiful all at the same time—when all of us all of the time really believe deep down that life is not about us but about God and God's work in the world?

Leaning into the Jesus Way
I was different after that day, for risking in a new way can be freeing. I had a new kind of desire to live closer to God—to "lean into the Jesus way," as I once heard a clergywoman friend describe this kind of resolve. Early in my ministry I really did not believe that I could be like Jesus because he seemed to call for too much, ask for more than I could do, and expect me to change too many of my ways. It felt like it was impossible—just too big a hill to climb. But something was shifting. I had climbed a hill, and instead of feeling fear and inadequacy, I began to see opportunity. I saw that my relationships could be so much better than they currently were. I saw that my church could be so much better. I really wanted that. People could learn to love more deeply. Finding this kind of depth in my own relationships was very appealing to me.

I no longer wanted to use all my energy holding on to the way things were; instead, I could put that energy into connecting, apologizing, forgiving, loving, and giving to others. And even more, I could step into God's presence right here, right now by moving out of my ego and letting go of status, power, privilege, and attachments to all kinds of so-called important things.

Was this what Bishop Muyombo was pointing to when he offered himself as a witness of all the good a worldwide church can do when it is serving God's purposes, not our own? Can people lay down their pride or anything that keeps them from serving God—like ego and the need to please others instead of God—so that they can connect with people all over the world who are doing the same thing? It is certainly not simple, but the bishop reminded me that day that people can truly live the abundant life that God intends for them and that everyone is offered this kind of opportunity.

Always Beginners, Always Equal

This abundant life, however, involves unlearning so many of our ways. I find it helpful to see our spiritual journeys as a series of concentric circles expanding out from a central core—not a linear pathway—so that each time I move along on a circle, I can go deeper, connect with God, and discover more clearly how God sees me—every part of me. During the spring of 2022, God gave me several opportunities to take a new look at myself and my tendency to over-value status and power.

As I heard testimonies from a few Alcoholic Anonymous and Al-Anon participants in the church and reread Richard Rohr's book, *Breathing Under Water: Spirituality and the Twelve Steps*, I was reminded that everyone has addictions. I saw my own addictions to being busy, to being right, to feeling important and powerful.

I recognized the status I enjoyed by being identified as ordained. Could I sometimes think I deserved a certain kind of respect in the church since I had studied and worked hard to get through many theological and psychological hurdles? Surely, I did not think I was somehow better than…

I began to see why Swiss theologian Karl Barth wrote how easy it is for clergy to forget that when it comes to their ultimate identity as a Christian, they are always beginners, always equals. It is not true that clergy are somehow better than other Christians just because they find themselves in a leadership position, in charge of church initiatives or programs.

I reflected on how I love to get people all fired up about my vision for a new program or a new way of doing church, and how I find great satisfaction in leading the charge. Nothing wrong with that. I have noticed, however, that it is more difficult for me to stay connected and be positive when parishioners choose—for some good reasons—to opt out of the "wonderful opportunity" I have given them to serve and be faithful.

I may need to forego more of my pride and ego and power and desire to be right. Oh, dear. Just when I thought I was making progress, I realized I have so much more work to do. There is so much more to learn, and I need to keep moving along that circle—in the right direction!

No wonder my colleague Paul Goodrich at Custer Road UMC told me to never push for a certain title or status at Lovers Lane. It is one of those statements I need to be reminded of again and again, especially when I feel insecure about something not going my way or am threatened by the success of a colleague. I need to discard many of my "ways of the world." Instead, I want to be authentic, remembering that my first calling is to love and serve others—not to be in charge of them. My calling is always to be present *with* others—not above them.

Flawed and Broken

I can only be real, live real, and love real when I acknowledge that I am both sinner and saint, good and bad. So is everyone. All people are good *and* bad. This truth—which at first seems like a contradiction—does not cancel one out over the other. You and I as human beings are living paradoxes, all of us.

Remember my first big spiritual breakthrough in Rabbi Olan's class on the human condition? Truth is found in paradox! Finally—at last—I saw that understanding this truth was the key to growing up spiritually, to going on the further journey.

As my Twelve Step friends have reinforced, if I am serious about my spiritual journey, I have to own that I am flawed, seriously flawed and broken. Much to my dismay, I still have all kinds of hang-ups, habits, and prejudices I need to be healed from. The good news is that everyone else has them, too. All of us are in the same boat. *And here's the really good news.* Jesus loved sinners. In fact, he sought them out. The people he got the most upset with—and this is important—were those who did NOT think they were sinners—like the Pharisees. He made some strong statements about them: "Woe to you, scribes and Pharisees, you hypocrites!" (Matthew 23:13 NRSV)

Let it soak in. God loves us *with* our hangups, our addictions, our reactive and out-of-balance behavior. He loves us anyway. As I had to hear clearly again that day at the waterfall in Kauai, God embraces all our imperfections. Why is it so hard for us to believe this? Most of us have the impression that we are supposed to be perfect in order for God to love us, but that is a lie. God loves everyone as they are—flawed. And once we embrace this, we are no longer separated from God.

Now that I really trust this kind of love, I can lay down my past, let go of what is holding me back, quit worrying about the future, and live fully in the present. This makes all the difference in the world. It is only in the present that God can meet me and connect with me—not in the past or future. In this space, nothing distracts me, the Kingdom breaks in. I am fully present to a God who is completely available to me.

I no longer have anything to protect or defend or prove. I am fully human and in touch with an all-powerful God. Nothing separates me from God. There are no distractions. I am no longer on the surface of life. I am living with the kind of intimacy that Jesus experienced with His Father. I am fully connected and fully present. This is about as good as it gets.

How wonderful it is to experience the true freedom that a further journey calls for and to have the kind of relationship with God in which I know I will not be judged, evaluated, manipulated, or used. I am loved fully, unconditionally, immediately, and without restriction.

It is perhaps equally shocking and sometimes very hard to believe that no one is superior to me or to anyone else. Jesus shows us again and again that there is absolutely nothing—no behavior or belief or lifestyle or religious activity—that can make anyone superior to anyone else. Our actions may be different, but in our essence, everyone is equally flawed—and equally loved.

I believe this kind of intimacy with God is the way everyone, ultimately, finds common ground with each other and finds meaning and purpose in their lives. I think it is what John Wesley was pointing to when he spoke of Christian perfection. I believe that this kind of encounter or experience is what the key characters in the Bible were all looking for, and it is what Jesus was speaking of when He said, "...I came that they may have life and have it abundantly."

(John 10:10 NRSV) Humility, honesty, and vulnerability are the traits that will get us there. *Get real, live real, love real.*

Living in the Present
As I look back over these 40-plus years serving two great churches, I celebrate the fact that I have been converted several times, hopefully moving toward transformation. Each change involves a letting go of the old and smaller self, so that I can bring in the new and more connected-to-God-and-others self—the capital S Self!

I now expect and believe that these spiritual breakthroughs will continue through my lifetime and beyond. I experienced one of these in the last four years as I took time to reflect and write. When I slowed down, clarity and wisdom came. These moments happened in spite of me—not because of me. I did not come seeking them, for I did not know how much I needed to be changed. I had the dangerous sin of contentment with the status quo. Thankfully, I had an open heart and a curious mind. These attributes, along with God's amazing grace, saved me.

Maybe my story as a woman is the story of all who are learning to stand on their own two feet while learning to love, listen to the Holy Spirit, and serve God in the places they find themselves in. I believe it is the story of a life of spiritual growth and becoming more fully human, and it is accessible to everyone. Through this process, I realize that I am hungry to find more companions, both women and men, who write and speak about this personal journey.

I have come to see that my calling is not just to go to lots of meetings, build buildings, manage programs, and start ministries. My deeper calling is to be a pastor, growing and learning, sitting with people like myself, being attentive to God speaking to me in my everyday life, and transforming me into someone who can be more human and holy.

I am so grateful for the visionary pastors of the two churches I have been honored to serve with, along with the strong lay people who were always faithful and wanted more—more for the church, more for people on the margins, more for the Kingdom. They helped me fall in love with Jesus again and again and to also fall in love with others.

I now see how blessed I have been on many different levels. I have experienced what it means to stand *with* and alongside men in my personal life (my father, my husband, my brother, my son, my grandsons), in my church life (colleagues), and in my community. I will stand up and promote this kind of mutual respect in relationships between women and men all around me.

I am so grateful to be a part of two United Methodist church families—two bodies of Christ—that truly accept and embrace women who are called to ministry and are grounded in a theology that rejects fear and any kind of resolve to "keep America Christian." I have had opportunities to stand with

Bringing Light

the Muslim brothers and sisters in my neighborhood, and I value—as well as respect—their meaningful contributions to the community.

I am grateful for the many gay (LGBTQ+) members at Lovers Lane and their strong leadership in our church. They tend to attend worship regularly; they serve and give and teach and lead while being available as mentors to those who have been excluded or made to feel less than. They bring light and faithfulness and authenticity to the Body, and while they know pain and rejection, I have never heard any of them dwell on the past. They are too busy worshiping and being thankful. They feed my soul.

I am also grateful for a growing number of refugees and immigrants in our community. One of those, Rocio Bamihe, swam the Rio Grande and entered Texas from Mexico when she was fifteen years old. Today, she serves as the director of our church nursery and helps with outreach and the Spanish-speaking service. She is presently pursuing the path to become a licensed local pastor in The United Methodist church—a sign of the future!

I am grateful to have been a part of life changes, conversions, and baptisms for young and old, poor and rich, deaf and hearing, black and white, gay and straight, alcoholics and sober—as all stepped into the same baptism waters. I expect this to continue in the future. I am grateful to have played a role in encouraging others to live out their calling, including a female worship leader named DeDe Jones who walked into my office at Lovers Lane one day and said excitedly, "I think I heard God speak to me in a dream last night and tell me, 'It is time for you to move to the front line.'" DeDe is now the Associate Pastor of Modern Worship and Evangelism at Lovers Lane and preaches each Sunday in Crosswalk, the most Spirit-led service I have ever been a part of.

Gender is no longer a big deal; isn't that wonderful? Recently, a male colleague named Joe Stobaugh, who today serves near me in a large church in Dallas, surprised me when he mentioned that I was the person who inspired him when I was at Custer Road UMC to pursue his call to full-time ministry. It's a new day!

My prayer is that *real* women and men of all kinds and races will continue to emerge, go inward, and learn to love and trust more, walk with and alongside—not lord over—others. I want to continue to grow and change, stretch, and have the courage to see the flawed and unbalanced sides of myself, my church, my country, and my world. I want to become friends with more immigrants, racial minorities, and non-Christians who have much to teach me. I want to go forward—not backward—by letting go more often. I want to be comfortable with listening more, not having to be right or certain.

I know what it means to live in fear, to live the lie that I am better than or superior to others whose life is not like mine. I know the prison that it puts me in, feeling the need to change others and make them more like me. Instead, I need to be more like *them* in some ways. I am resolved to stay free and to help others who suffer with any kind of superiority.

I want to stand up against power that desires to dominate and control; instead, I want to encourage the kind of inner power through the Holy Spirit that lifts everyone up. I want to be a member and a leader in The United Methodist Church that is emerging in this century—a more diverse and authentic church that listens more deeply and loves all into a relationship with Jesus. I want to help heal wounds from so much of the division in the country and world today. I want to follow Jesus.

Everybody Belongs, Everything Is Connected

Since God's love for all is right here, right now in our midst (when everyone lives in the present), no one is ever left out, less than, set apart, uninvited, or rejected. *Everything and everyone belongs!* People are connected to each other and to everything else in nature, the universe, the world. Nothing stands alone. No one feels insecure; all feel loved.

This kind of love is available for everyone. God has a heart that cares for all the people in the world. "For God so loved the world…" (John 3:16 NRSV)

He does not favor people with certain skin colors or political beliefs. He does not favor certain countries or nationalities. God makes it clear that He loves all people.

This truth is amazing! All people are human beings on a spiritual journey together trying to figure out what it means to be fully human and to know God. People begin by knowing who they are—sinners in need of grace, good people who sometimes do not-so-good things, beautiful people who are broken. They know that God is real and that He wants to have an encounter with every person.

People then walk with and alongside others, moving forward together, acknowledging that they need a power greater than themselves. They go inward, listen to God, and are always beginners. They remain curious and open; they are influenced by and learn from others. They live in the present and are forever young. They forgive and stand up and stand in for those who need them. They proclaim Jesus over manipulation and control. They find their souls. They live differently. They search for God's activity all around them and join God in redeeming the world. They pay attention and become friends with people on the margins.

Non-Negotiable Belief

I acknowledge that people are at different places in their spiritual journeys and come to different conclusions, but there is one belief that is non-negotiable for me—that I can't budge on. Everyone is equally made in the image of God; everyone is equal at the foot of the cross—no exceptions. This core belief sits at the heart of my theology. I am not alone.

For example, in Acts 10:34-36 (NRSV), Peter says: "I truly understand that God shows no partiality, but in every nation, anyone who fears him, and practices righteousness is acceptable to him. You know the message he sent to the people of Israel; preaching peace by Jesus Christ—he is Lord of all." I also believe that this means I cannot grow into the full image of God given to me until I interact with people who have different backgrounds and different views than I do.

Many of the Bible stories remind us that *all* are children of God, e.g., the Good Samaritan, Mary and Martha, the Ethiopian eunuch. They point us to the deeper truth that differences are good, and that the "least of these" has the most to teach. Jesus is very clear about any kind of desire to separate from others. Again and again through his teaching and way of relating to others, he shows us that walls and divisions don't work. There is always more than enough space, resources, or room to provide for everyone—as illustrated in the stories of the two fishes and the wedding wine. God is clearly a God of abundance, not scarcity—of love, not indifference.

If you or I allow the deep space inside us to be filled with darkness or fear instead of the light of the Holy Spirit, separation from others is the result. The Holy Spirit always connects rather than divides.

The Holy Spirit enables human beings to embrace their imperfections. They no longer have to be certain or right. They know they are not perfect; like everyone else, they are complex, flawed, and beautiful. They are loved as they are, becoming who God calls them to be—all people, each one. When there is conflict and tension, the most mature or most secure and feeling-loved person in the room speaks up to find common ground and connection.

No more separation.

Giving Back Our Greatest Gift

Now I know that every ordinary life can be extraordinary.

We can float along, drifting here and there, or we can use our given lifetime to discover and live out our True Self—our unique destiny. It is not something we *can* do or *should* do; it is something we *must* do. Otherwise, our own little bit of heaven that God has given us goes missing. Right? Can we see this? Everyone is worse because of it. Most of all, we are worse off, because our Self—with a capital S–is unduplicable. It will never appear again in our own unique form. This soul print, as Pastor Mark Batterson calls it, is given to us at birth. Let that sink in; it is God-given. One time only. No do-overs.

I hope you have a sense of urgency about this. I know I do. Awakening to our True Self is the best part of going on the further journey. Of course, most of this does not come easily or without bumps in the road. It is given to us when we are ready; we don't earn it. Our part is to say, "Ah-ha!" "Oh, yes!" "Wow!" For we do not get to make our souls; we just get to help grow them up, and this process starts by unlearning much of what we have been taught by the world.

The beautiful part of this journey is that we can go to the top of the top of the top of the mountain with others—with spiritual companions who beckon us forward, encouraging us, inspiring us, and holding our hand.

We will discover together that the greatest gift we can give—to each other and to God—is the gift of ourselves!

Once we uncover this truest Self—the place where we know we are born out of God's love and that God loved us first and unconditionally—then we are free to love others unconditionally and with a divine kind of love. We can even love our enemies! We are transformed.

I believe this is the way God relates to the world; we give back to Him what He first gave us—our unique, truest Self.

Jesus' words to his disciples in John 13:34-35 ring true: "I am giving you a new commandment that you love one another. Just as I have loved you, you should love each other.

Your love for one another will prove to the world that you are my disciples."

Voice of Hope and Truth and Goodness
In much the same way, every church can be extraordinary; it has a unique and God-given mission to fulfill—a gift to give back to God. Every church can take its ordinary story and make an extraordinary impact on the community and beyond, for the Church's message to the world has never been more needed. The message is one of hope for the future, NOT fear, of optimism, NOT despair, of truth, NOT confusion. God's message to the world that He loves us has not changed. We serve a God who is constantly working to bring about good in every situation, a God who is ultimately in charge of it all. "And we know that in all things God works for the good of those who love him…" (Galatians 8:28) The message of the book of Revelation and of the New Testament is good news, not bad news, for with God, good ultimately wins out.

This message of hope and truth is especially needed today in our current American climate. Due to a variety of reasons, including social media, the over-all political climate, the amount of change going on, and the feeling among many that someone is losing if someone else is winning, many Americans have started to believe that things are much worse than they actually are. Since this does not square with the studies that show people are better off in most ways in this generation than any other generation before, it is clear that many people seem to prefer to believe the opposite. Some of these are in the church. Frank Bruni in his book *The Age of Grievance* says that it has become almost popular to go against the grain, to use hurtful words, to not be able to discern between minor and major grievances, to have Individuals play the victim card and blame others instead of taking responsibility for their choices.

It is easy to lose perspective, and I find this to be the opposite of what God is calling His churches to be and to encourage. Jesus makes it clear he came to bring life, not death, and our churches must find their truest and deepest voice—the voice of hope and faith for our future.

At its core, the way we view our circumstances is influenced by the way we view God. The church needs to continually speak of who God is—a good God who wants the best for us and is available to help us in every part of our life. The United Methodist church—and other churches living out God's calling—have a word to scream to the mountaintops about the negative thinking going on in the world. Fear and anger and anxiety do NOT have the last word; hope and love and faithfulness and abundance do.

May we celebrate the fact that the church which Jesus instituted more than 2,000 years ago is the same church today from which we proclaim to our communities the goodness of God, the faithfulness of God, the presence of God—every day, every hour, every moment.

We can then join God and participate with Him in His work in the world as we keep moving forward in faith, giving up our childish and immature ways, remembering and celebrating the love that He first gave us and that we now give back in return. Our message to the community and the world remains the same: the greatest power of all is found in the real, authentic, unconditional, never-ending love of a God who provides what we need and more. "God is able to provide you with every blessing in abundance, so that by always having enough of everything, you may share abundantly in every good work." (2 Corinthians 9:8)

You are enough!

I am enough!

We are enough—together!

Epilogue

David Faulkner Edwards died in February of 1946, eight months before I was born in October of that year.

A death occurs; a baby arrives; an ending is followed by a beginning. It seems to be part of the rhythm of life, one way God works.

I wish I had known David.

Like him, I certainly like bright and vivid colors. I've always been a voracious reader. I also enjoy being involved in politics, both local and national, as well as on the church level.

He was a beloved statesman who served four terms in the Louisiana House of Representatives. He represented West Carroll Parish, which includes my hometown of Kilbourne in the northeast corner of the state, continuously from 1924 to 1940. He never allowed politics to interfere with decisions and always voted his conscience.

Listening to Aunt Bee, it was dawning on me that I was like him in many ways, and I admired his character and his integrity.

I was beginning to see him as a kind of confidant, passing on to me his curiosity, love of politics, love of words, interest in language and stories, optimistic spirit, desire for a strong inner life, and yearning for more than a small town could offer.

I loved discovering this strong connection with him. What a joy!

When David died, Aunt Bee said it was a big loss for our family—with much grief for those who knew and loved him.

I'll always be grateful, however, for the timeless gift David's life gave me; I can now fully embrace, maybe for the first time, that awkward teenage girl who didn't belong in rural confines, who was no good at farming or anything mechanical, but who passionately loved learning. David was the soulmate I never met.

"Aunt Bee, tell me more about my grandfather."

A 2002 portrait depicting four generations of strong women, starting with my mother Norine (top right), me (top left), my daughter Wendi (center), and her daughter Hailey (bottom right).

Senior Pastor Stan Copeland and I pose together in the sanctuary of Lovers Lane United Methodist Church in 2023.

The sanctuary of Lovers Lane United Methodist Church is the largest stained glass building in the United States. The colors in the glass symbolize upward movement toward the Holy Spirit.

My cottage in Chandler, Texas, adjoined by a soothing pond, sits on 25 acres of land surrounded by the piney hills of East Texas.

Don and I celebrate our 58th Christmas together in 2023.

Family photo taken Christmas 2023. Standing left to right: Kamryn Sanchez (granddaughter), Pierce Sanchez (grandson), Bryan Sanchez (son-in-law), Hailey Sanchez (granddaughter), Wendi Sanchez (daughter), me, Don, Landry Whitehead (granddaughter), Kylie Whitehead (daughter-in-law), Hayden (granddaughter), Drake (grandson), Trey (son).

Don and his nephew, Lance Black, share family memories together in Lovers Lane sanctuary. Lance wrote the screenplay for Milk (2008), earning him the Academy Award for Best Original Screenplay.

My grandfather, David Faulkner Edwards, was a beloved statesman. He was self-taught and went on to serve four terms in the Louisiana House of Representatives. He represented West Carroll Parish, which includes my hometown of Kilbourne in the northeast corner of the state, continuously from 1924 to 1940. He never allowed politics to interfere with decisions and always voted his conscience.

Acknowledgments

I am convinced that gratitude is the healthiest emotion of all, and I am deeply grateful for the help and support I received from others to write this book. Getting started and believing I could do this was the hardest part, so God sent me help along the way.

About five years ago, Lucinda Holmes, a friend from seminary days, started me in the right direction when I ran into her in the bookstore at The Church of the Resurrection in Kansas City. "When are you going to write a book?" she said. "You do remember that you were the best writer in our class at Perkins, don't you?"

"No, I don't remember that," I said. Her comment, however, started me thinking. It seemed to bring to life that part of me that wanted—even needed—to write.

As I was struggling with what to write about, my friend, DeDe Jones, who loves the church as much as I do, said, "You must write about the church—about your faith journey." *Really? Is my faith journey worth writing about?* I was not convinced at all, but thank you, DeDe.

So, I started—just started. It seemed to take forever and certainly did not come easily. I needed honesty from friends. My friend, Barbara Marcum, was real enough to say to me about one part of an early chapter, "I am not connecting to this part." She found another part and said, "This is it; this is good." I was relieved and began to understand my writing style more. Slowly I moved forward. My sister, Diane Grantham, got excited about helping me with our early family history and gave me encouragement.

When I finished what I thought was my final draft—I was so naïve—almost three years ago, and gave it to Julie Cantrell, a gifted, well-known writer who became a friend and encourager, Julie was kind but firm. She helped me see that I was writing a memoir that should read by everyone instead of a study resource to be ready by only women, and she let me know that it needed quite a bit of work. Did I have the courage to face and write about the not-so-good parts of my life along with the easier parts? It was a turning point.

More than a year later, I got the "kick-in-the-pants" I needed from a friend, Cathy, who read the script and gave it a kind of blessing by comparing it to a rather well-known inspirational writer, Joel Osteen. I was surprised but encouraged. That, along with support from a family member and well-known writer, Dustin Lance Black, was what I needed at that point.

Acknowledgments

The one friend who was a constant during the entire five years or more was Tori Barlow, who said "Yes" to me as I changed course again and again. She acted as if that was normal and a good thing. She knew that finishing the book was important to me, and she did not want me to give up.

A big, big thank you to my family—my husband, Don, who has supported me not only through this writing time but through all my ministry; my daughter and son, Wendi and Trey; their spouses, Bryan and Kylie; and then, of course, the six grandchildren, Hailey, Pierce, Kamryn, Landry, Hayden, and Drake. How do I express the kind of deep and incredible love I feel for them? They have loved me back, even though I have not always been the kind of wife, mother, and grandmother they might have preferred. Grace abounds.

I am grateful for Mark Craig, Paul Goodrich, and Stan Copeland, the three United Methodist pastors who stood alongside me as a woman in ministry in a time when this was often criticized and not widely accepted. They never wavered in their support and treated me as a partner; they had my back, a gift that is invaluable. I was blessed.

I am grateful to all the friends, lay people, and staff in the two congregations—Custer Road United Methodist Church and Lovers Lane United Methodist Church—who are still teaching me how to be a pastor. They are too numerous to name, and they remain a part of this journey with me.

I am thankful to Stan Copeland, also, for giving me insights about writing along the way and who was the first person to say to me, "This is publishable." Thanks go to Mary Reed and Joan Gray LaBarr, who served as editors, along with Beth Emery, Royanne Kerr, Barbara Lemmon, Dallas Swan, Shannon Watson, and Sherrie and Rusty George, who were encouragers along the way. Bruce Ryrie prayed for me throughout the long process, especially when I was stuck. Your prayers meant so much, Bruce!

Incredible gratitude goes to Chris Kelley and Mac Boles who believed in the book and definitely got me over the finish line. Without their shaping and editing and encouragement and more editing, I never could have finished the book!

Most of all, I am thankful for that inner voice within each of us, the Holy Spirit, that kept telling me to get out of my ego and just write.

About the Author

Donna Whitehead is the Associate Pastor of Lovers Lane United Methodist Church in Dallas, Texas, where she has faithfully served the diverse, historic congregation for 24 years. One of the first seven women to be ordained by the North Texas UMC Conference, Donna has served in Christian ministry for 44 years as a pastor and United Methodist conference leader. Her pioneering spirit led her to become one of the first women enrolled at the Perkins School of Theology, the first female intern at Highland Park United Methodist Church in 1979, the first female chair of the Plano Ministerial Alliance in 1985, the first female chair of the Finance and Administration Team for the North Texas UMC Conference in 1988, and the first full-time director for the Lovers Lane United Methodist Church Foundation in 2004. She was featured in Dina Moor's book, *Unstoppable Woman* (Case Books), published in 2008.

Her first 20 years of ministerial success as an associate pastor at Custer Road United Methodist Church, where she helped build the congregation from the ground up, made her an authority on church growth and lay leadership development. She has taught workshops around the country about how to grow churches and is known for her work in starting classes and small groups—including those promoting the Bethel Bible Study, the Alpha course, the Experiencing God Series, and most recently *The Chosen* series.

She holds a bachelor's degree from the University of North Texas, a master's degree from Southern Methodist University, and a master's in divinity from the Perkins School of Theology at SMU.

She and her husband, Don Whitehead, have been married for 59 years. They reside in Plano, Texas, and have two adult children and six grandchildren.

Recommended Reading

Barnhouse, Ruth Tiffany. Identity; Know Yourself in the Image of God. Philadelphia: The Westminster Press, 1984.

Blackaby, Henry and Richard and Claude V. King. Experiencing God; Knowing and Doing the will of God, Revised and Expanded. Nashville: R&H Publishing Group, 2008, 2021.

Brown, Barbara Taylor. Leaving Church; A Memoir of Faith. New York: Harper Collins, 2006.

Bruni, Frank. The Age of Grievance. Jackson, TN: Simon & Schuster, 2024.

Chilcote, Paul W. She Offered Them Christ; The Legacy of Women Preachers in Early Methodism. Nashville: Abingdon Press, 1993.

Du Mez, Kristen Kobes. Jesus and John Wayne; How White Evangelicals Corrupted a Faith and Fractured a Nation. New York: Liveright Publishing Corporation, 2020.

Friday, Nancy. My Mother, My Self; The Daughter's Search for Identity. New York: Dell Publishing Company, 1977.

Hatmaker, Jen. Fierce, Free, and Full of Fire; The Guide to Being Glorious You. Nashville: Nelson Books, 2020.

Moore, Beth. All My Knotted-Up Life; A Memoir. Tyndale, 2023.

Moore, Henry. The Life of Mrs. Mary Fletcher, Consort and Relict of the Rev. John Fletcher. Nicholasville, Kentucky: Schmul Publishing Company, 1977.

Elizabeth O'Conner. Our Many Selves; A Handbook for Self-Discovery. New York: Harper and Row, 1971.

Peck, Scott. Further Along the Road Less Traveled; The Unending Journey Toward Spiritual Growth. New York: Walker and Company, 1993.

Peterson, Eugene. The Pastor. Harper One, 2011.

Rohr, Richard. Breathing Under Water; Spirituality and the Twelve Steps. Cincinnati: Franciscan Media, 2011.

Rohr, Richard. Falling Upward; A Spirituality for the Two Halves of Life. San Francisco: Jossey-Bass, 2011.

Sheehy, Gail. Passages; Predictable Crises of Adult Life. New York: Banton Books, 1974.

Vancil, Marilyn. Self to Lose; Self to Find; A Biblical Approach to the 9 Enneagram Types. Redemption Press, 2016.

Willimon, Will. Accidental Preacher; A Memoir. Grand Rapids, Michigan: William B. Eerdmans Publishing Company, 2019.

Made in the USA
Columbia, SC
02 October 2024